Gainsborough:
151 Paintings and Drawings

By Maria Tsaneva

First Edition

*****

I0474583

Gainsborough: 151 Paintings and Drawings
*****

Foreword

Thomas Gainsborough (1727 – 1788) was an English portrait and landscape artist, the most versatile English painter of the 18th century. He was the most inventive and original, always prepared to experiment with new ideas and techniques. Gainsborough alone among the great portrait painters of the era also devoted serious attention to landscapes. Unlike Reynolds, he was no great believer in an academic tradition and laughed at the fashion for history painting; an instinctive painter, he delighted in the poetry of paint. In his racy letters Gainsborough shows a warm-hearted and generous character and an independent mind. His comments on his own work and methods, as well as on some of the old masters, are very revealing and throw considerable light on contemporary views of art. Gainsborough was noted for the speed with which he applied paint, and he worked more from observations of nature than from application of formal academic rules. The poetic sensibility of his paintings caused Constable to say, "On looking at them, we find tears in our eyes and know not what brings them." His later work was characterized by a light palette and easy, economical strokes.

Gainsborough was the youngest son of John Gainsborough, a maker of woolen goods. When he was 13, he persuaded his father to send him to London to study on the strength of his promise at landscape.

He worked as an assistant to Hubert Gravelot, a French painter and engraver and an important figure in London art circles at the time. From him Gainsborough learned something of the French Rococo expression, which had a considerable influence on the development of his style. In 1746 in London he married Margaret Burr, the illegitimate daughter of the Duke of Beaufort. Soon afterward he returned to Suffolk and settled in Ipswich in 1752; his daughters Mary and Margaret were born in 1748 and 1752, respectively. In Ipswich Gainsborough met his first biographer, Philip Thicknesse. He early acquired some reputation as a portrait and landscape painter and made an adequate living.

Gainsborough declared that his first love was landscape and began to learn the language of this art from the Dutch 17th-century landscapists, who by 1740 were becoming popular with English collectors; his first landscapes were influenced by Jan Wynants.

But by 1748, when he painted Cornard Wood, Jacob van Ruisdael had become the predominant influence; although it is full of naturalistic detail, Gainsborough probably never painted directly from nature. He anticipates the realism of the great English landscapist of the next century, John Constable, but for the most part fancy held sway. In many of the early landscapes the influence of Rococo design learned from Gravelot is evident, together with a feeling for the French pastoral tradition. Although Gainsborough preferred landscape, he knew he must paint portraits for economic reasons. He painted few full-length portraits in Suffolk. Mr. William Woollaston, although an ambitious composition, is intimate and informal.

To obtain a wider public, Gainsborough moved in 1759 to Bath, where his studio was soon thronged with fashionable sitters. He moved in musical and theatrical circles, and among his friends were members of the Linley family, whose portraits he painted. At Bath he also met the actor David Garrick, for whom he had a profound admiration and whom he painted on many occasions. His passion for music and the stage continued throughout his life. In spite of the demand for portraits, he continued to paint landscapes.

In 1761 he sent a portrait of Earl Nugent to the Society of Artists, and in the following year the first notice of his work appeared in the London press. Throughout the 1760s he exhibited regularly in London and in 1768 was elected a foundation member of the Royal Academy. Characteristically he never took much part in the deliberations.

In Bath, Gainsborough had to satisfy a more sophisticated clientele and adopted a more formal and elegant portrait style based largely on a study of Van Dyck at Wilton, where he made a free copy of Van Dyck's painting of the Pembroke family. By 1769, when he painted Isabella Countess of Sefton, it is easy to see the refining influence of Van Dyck in the dignified simplicity of the design and the subtle muted colouring. One of Gainsborough's most famous pictures, The Blue Boy, was probably painted in 1770. In painting this subject in Van Dyck dress, he was following an 18th-century fashion in painting, as well as doing homage to his hero. The influence of Van Dyck is most clearly seen in the more official portraits.

In 1774 Gainsborough moved to London and settled in part of Schomberg House in Pall Mall. Fairly soon he began to be noticed by the royal family and partly because of his informality and Tory politics was preferred by George III above the official court painter, Sir Joshua Reynolds. In 1781 he was commissioned to paint the King and Queen.

In London Gainsborough continued his landscape work. In 1783 he made an expedition to the Lake District to see for himself the wild scenery extolled by the devotees of the picturesque. On his return he painted a number of mountain scenes that have analogies with the work of Gaspard Dughet, whose works were widely distributed in English country houses. Some sea pieces dating from the 1780s show a new kind of realism, harking back to the Dutch seascape tradition. During his last years Gainsborough was haunted by his nostalgia for Arcadia in the English countryside and painted a series of pictures of peasant life more ideal than real.

He died in 1788 and was buried in Kew churchyard.

Paintings and Drawings

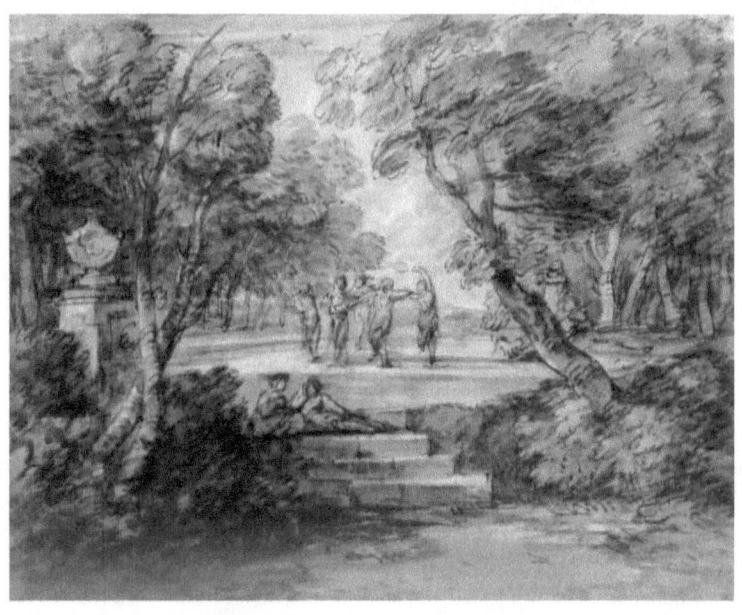

Dancers with Musicians in a Woodland Glade, 1733, chalk

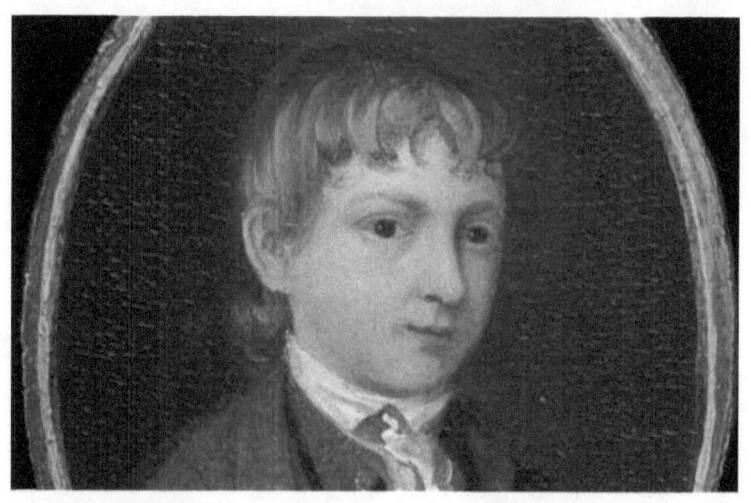

The miniature portrait of a young boy (supposed self-portrait), c.1737, oil

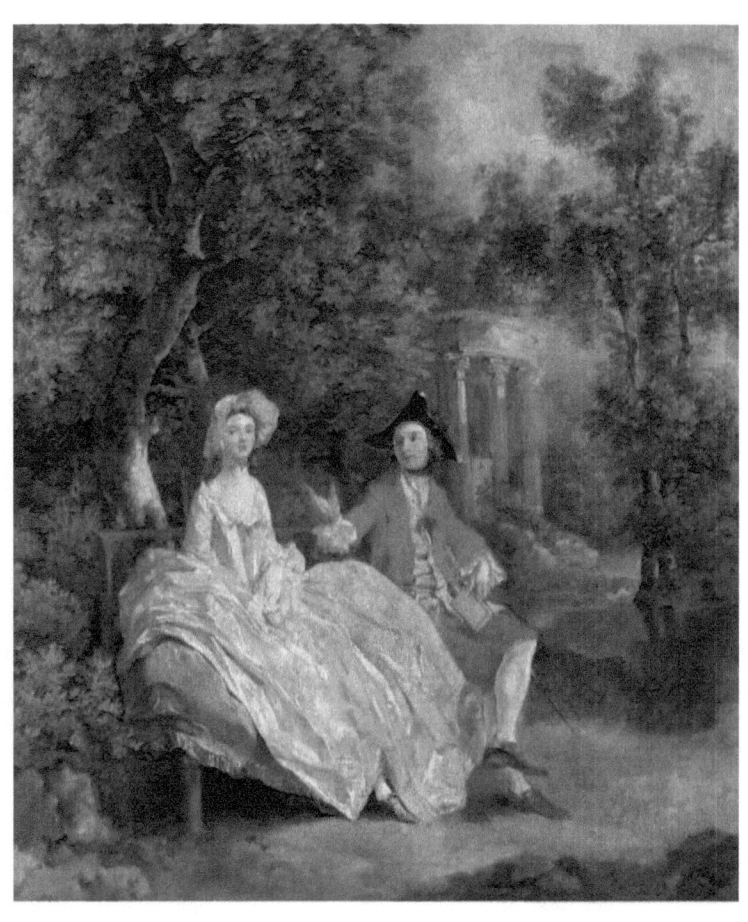

Conversation in a Park, 1745, oil on canvas

This charming picture belongs to Gainsborough's early period, when he was working in London and Suffolk. The theme of the conversation in a park evokes Watteau and his school; it denotes a French influence, which played a considerable part in the formation of the artist - he was in fact a pupil of the French engraver Gravelot at the St Martins Lane Academy. This picture has been thought to represent Thomas Sandby and his wife. At the Watson sale in 1832, it was described as depicting the artist and his wife. The painter's marriage took place in 1746; a very similar work, Mr and Mrs Andrews, is dated 1748.

The open-air portrait is a familiar theme in the English school, whereas in eighteenth-century France the portrait is usually in an interior. The evocation of nature by the English portrait painters is on the whole conventional; it is quite another matter with Gainsborough, however, who has treated the landscape for its own sake.

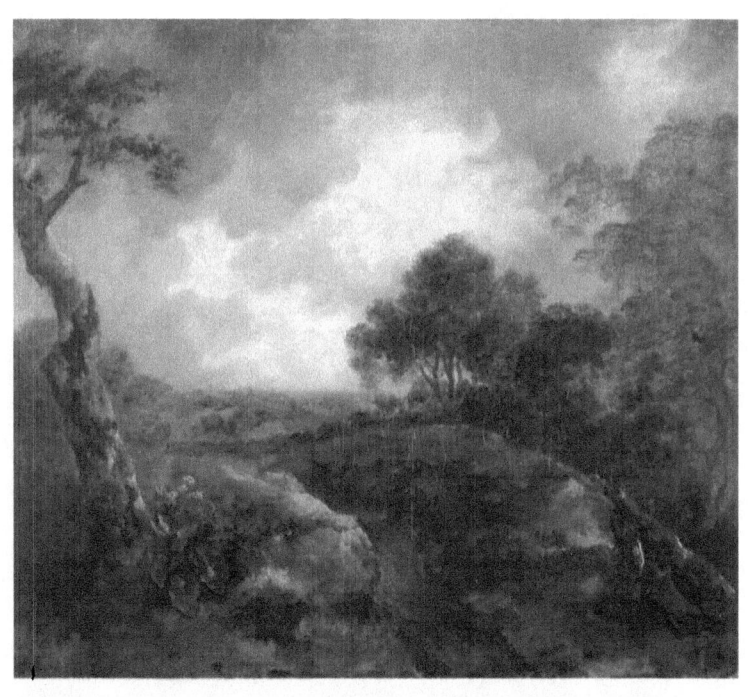

Open Landscape at the Edge of a Wood, 1745, oil on canvas

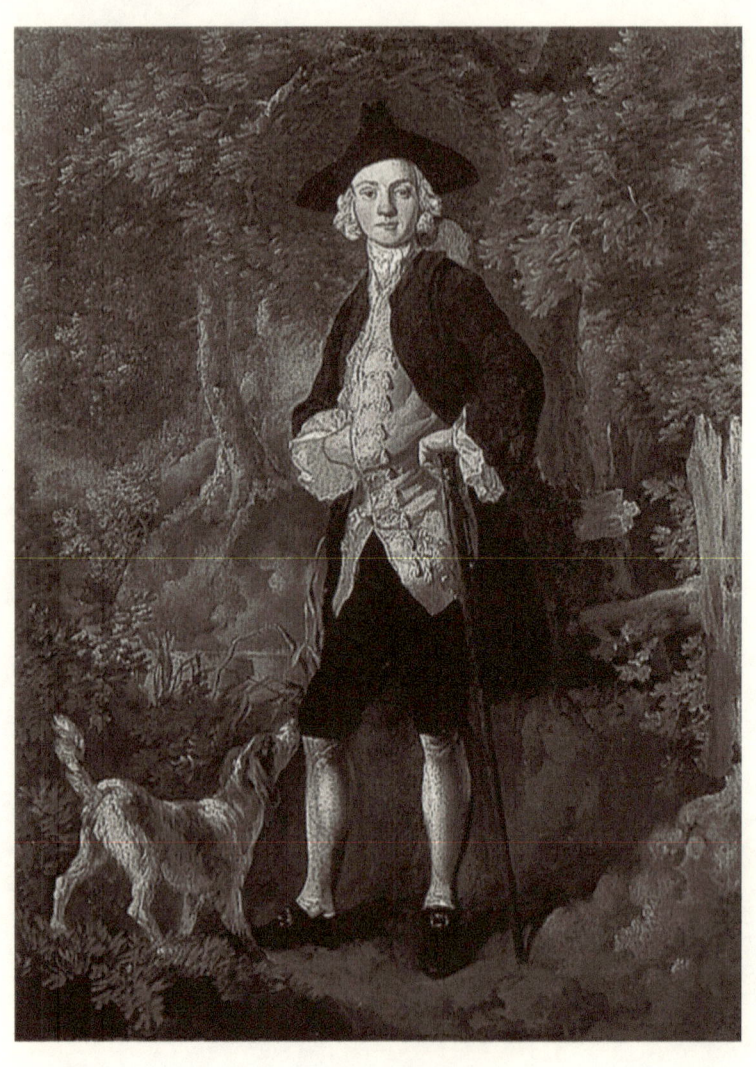

Man with a Dog in a Wood, 1746, oil on canvas

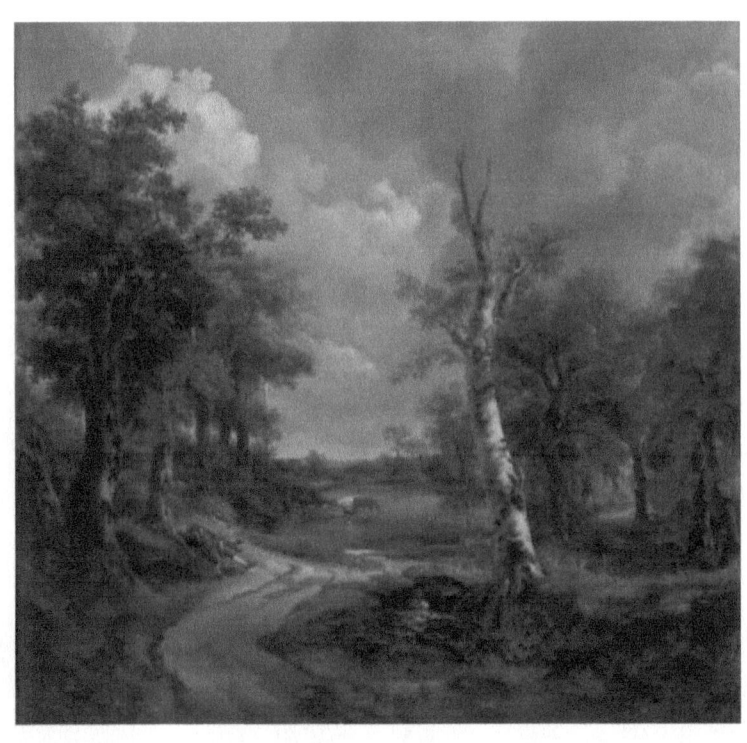

Drinkstone Park (Cornard Woodland), c.1747, oil

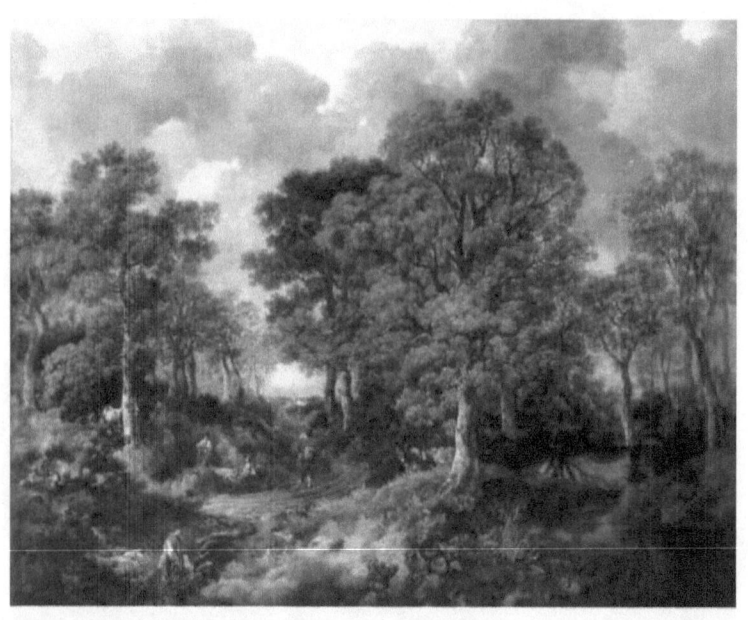

Forest (Cornard Wood), 1747, oil on canvas

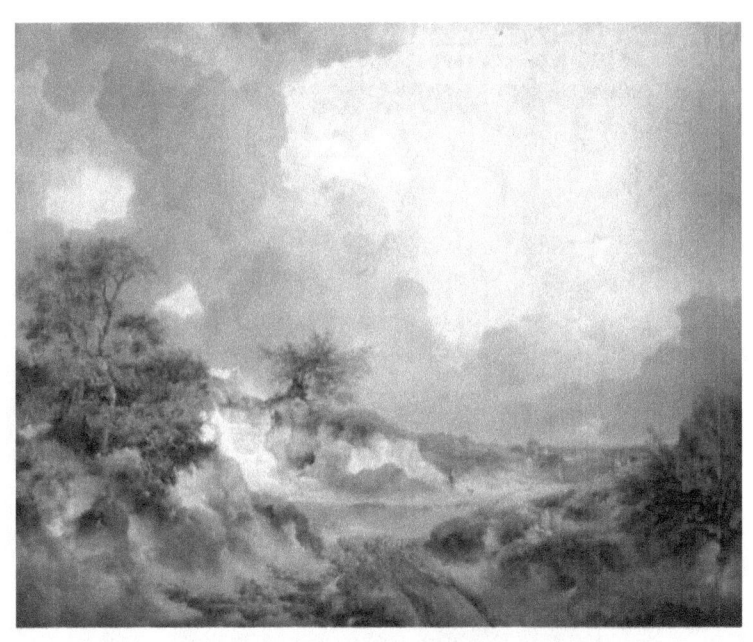

Landscape with Sandpit, 1747, oil on canvas

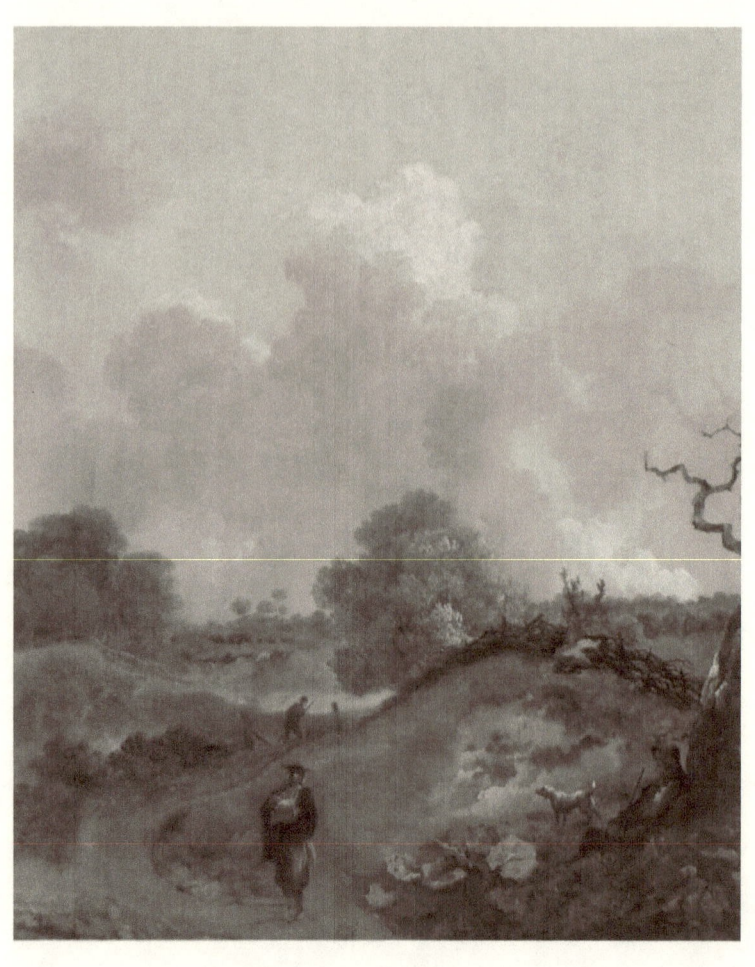

A country road, 1747, oil on canvas

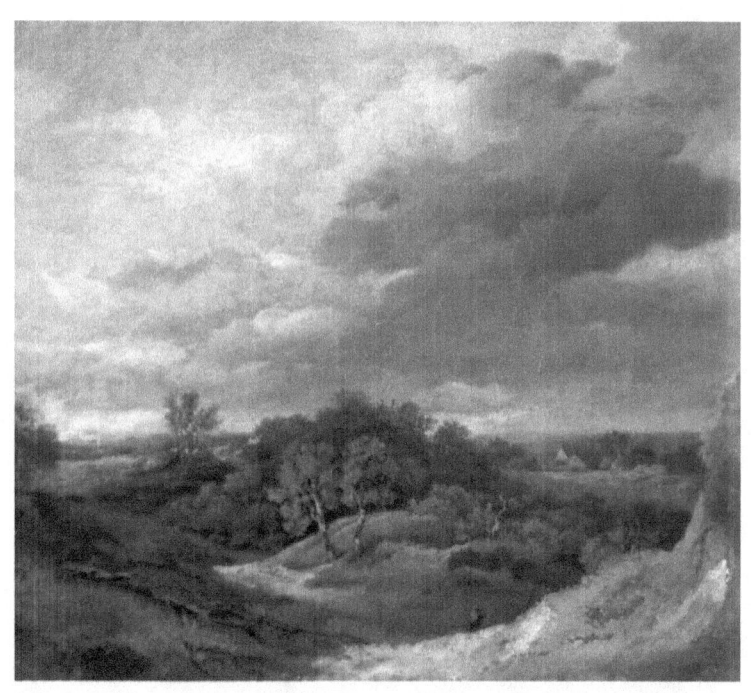

Landscape, 1747, oil on canvas

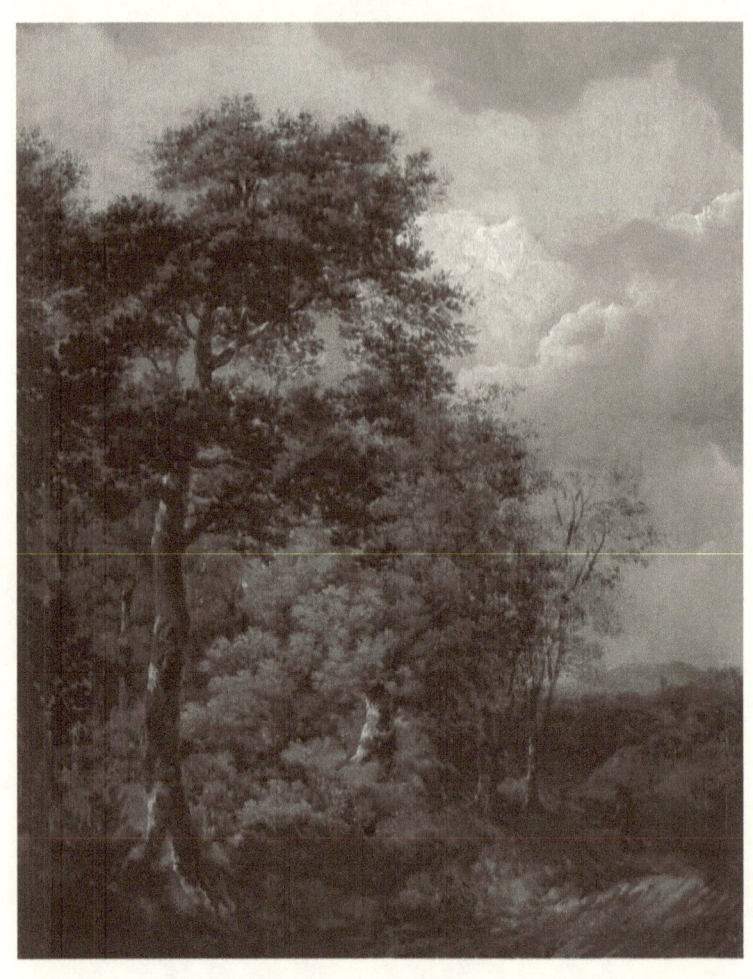

Landscape with a Peasant on a Path, 1747, oil on canvas

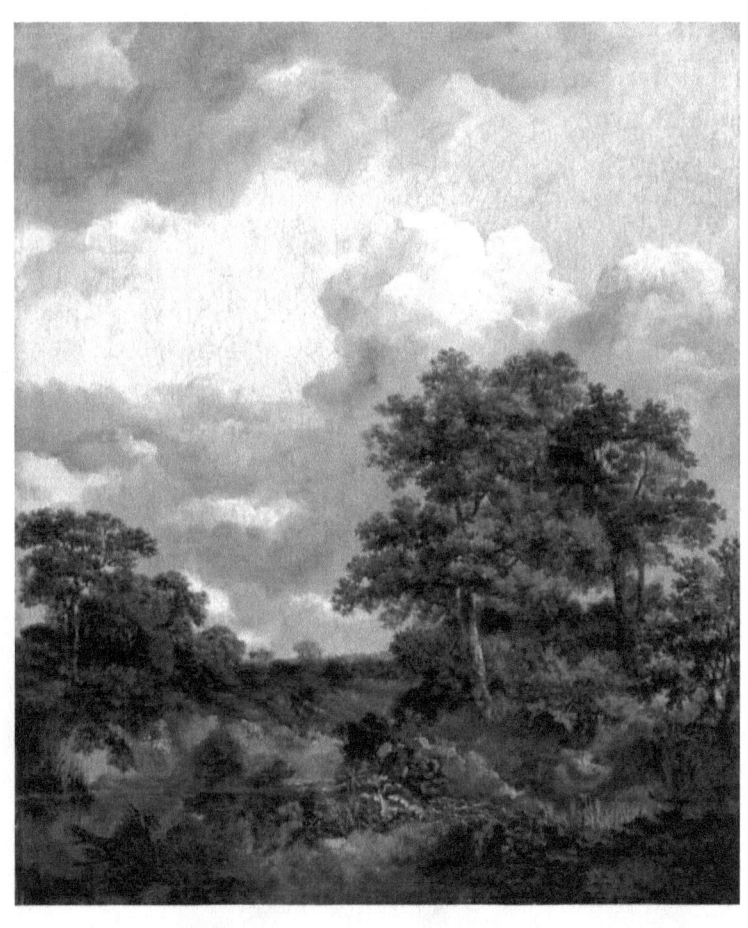

Landscape with a Pool, 1747, oil on canvas

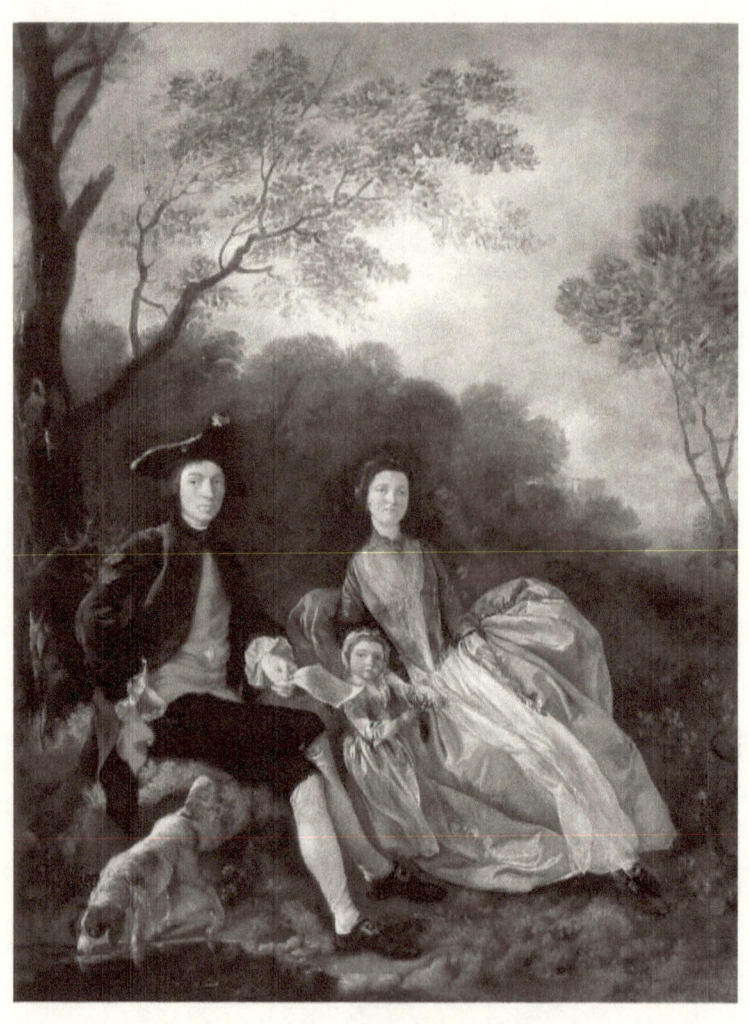

The Artist with his Wife and Daughter, 1748, oil on canvas

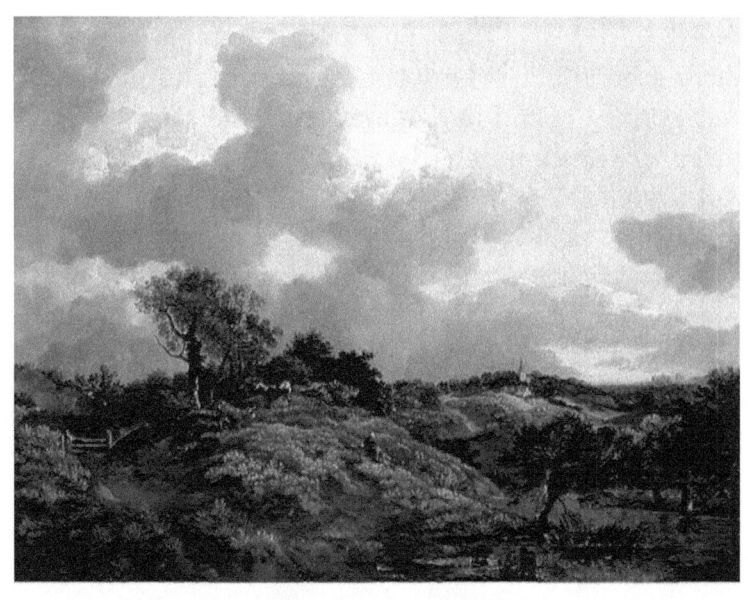

Wooded Landscape with a Herdsman Seated, 1748, oil on canvas

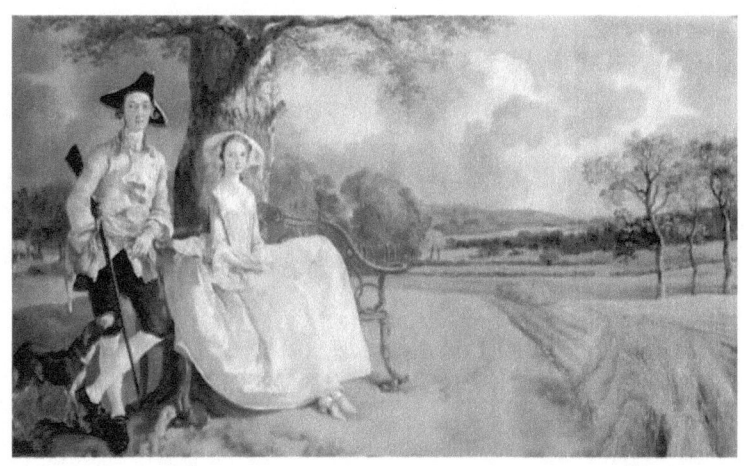

Mr. and Mrs. Andrews, 1749, oil on canvas

Robert Andrews and his wife Frances Mary, were married in 1748, not long before Gainsborough painted their portraits - and that of Auberies, their farm near Sudbury. The church in the background is St Peter's, Sudbury, and the tower to the left is that of Lavenham church. The small full-length portrait in an open-air rustic setting is typical of Gainsborough's early works, painted in his native Suffolk after his return from London; the identifiable view is unusual, and may have been specified by the patrons. We must not imagine that they sat together under a tree while Gainsborough set up his easel among the sheaves of corn; their costumes were most likely painted from dressed-up artist's mannequins, which may account for their doll-like appearance, and the landscape would have been studied separately.

This kind of picture, commissioned by people 'who lived in rooms which were neat but not spacious', in Ellis Waterhouse's happy phrase about Gainsborough's contemporary Arthur Devis, was a speciality of painters who were not 'out of the top drawer'. The sitters, or their mannequin stand-ins, are posed in 'genteel attitudes' derived from manuals of manners. The nonchalant Mr Andrews, fortunate possessor of a game licence, has his gun under his arm; Mrs Andrews, ramrod straight and neatly composed, may have been meant to hold a book, or, it has been suggested, a bird which her husband has shot. In the event, a reserved space left in her lap has not been filled in with any identifiable object.

Out of these conventional ingredients Gainsborough has composed the most tartly lyrical picture in the history of art. Mr Andrews's satisfaction in his well-kept farmlands is as nothing to the intensity of the painter's feeling for the gold and green of fields and copses, the supple curves of fertile land meeting the stately clouds. The figures stand out brittle against that glorious yet ordered bounty. But how marvellously the acid blue hooped skirt is deployed, almost, but not quite, rhyming with the curved bench back, the pointy silk shoes in sly communion with the bench feet, while Mr Andrews's substantial shoes converse with tree roots. (The faithful gun dog had better watch out for his unshod paws.) More rhymes and assonances link the lines of gun, thighs, dog, calf, coat; a coat tail answers the hanging ribbon of a sun hat; something jaunty in the husband's tricorn catches the corner of his wife's eye. Deep affection and naive artifice combine to create the earliest successful depiction of a truly English idyll.

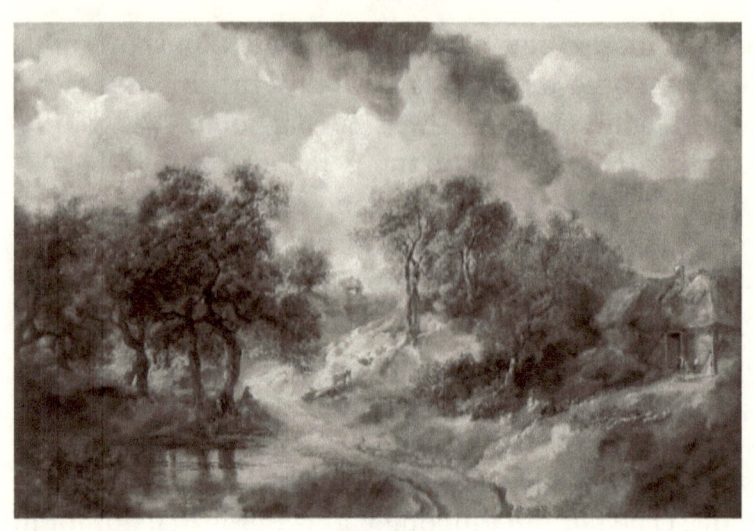

Landscape in Suffolk, 1750, oil on canvas

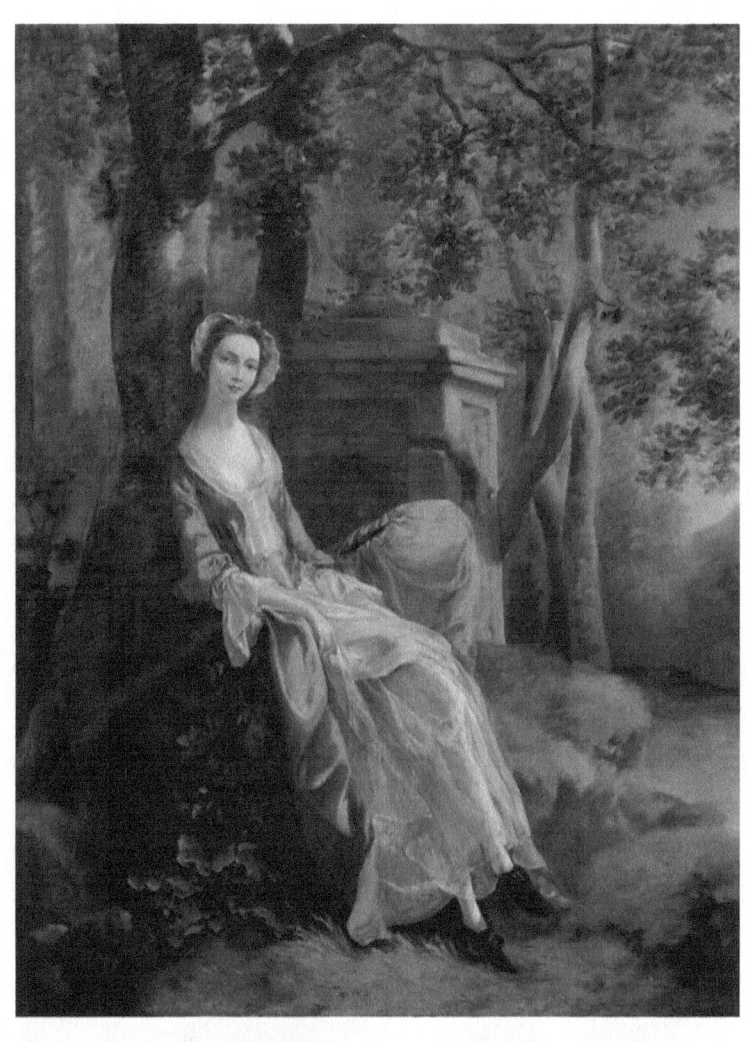

Portrait of a Woman (possibly of the Lloyd Family),
1750, oil on canvas

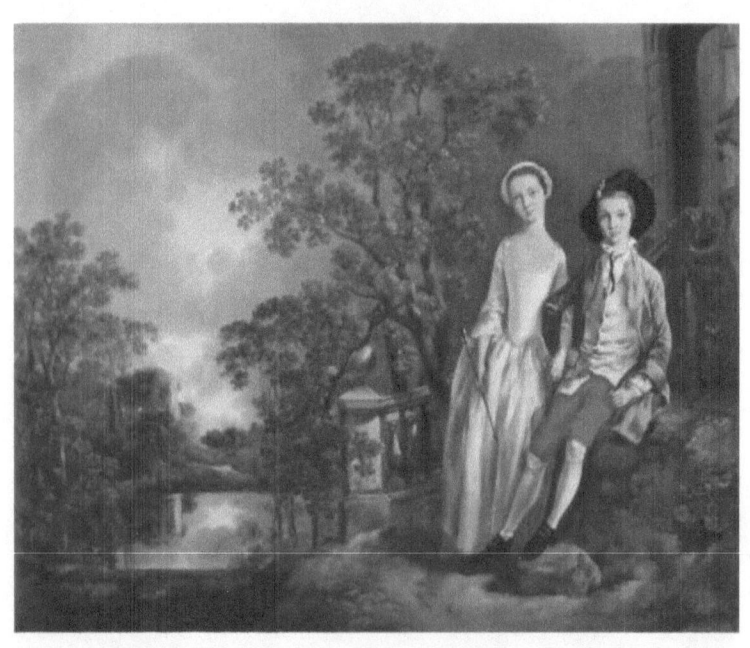

Portrait of Heneage Lloyd and his Sister, Lucy, 1750, oil on canvas

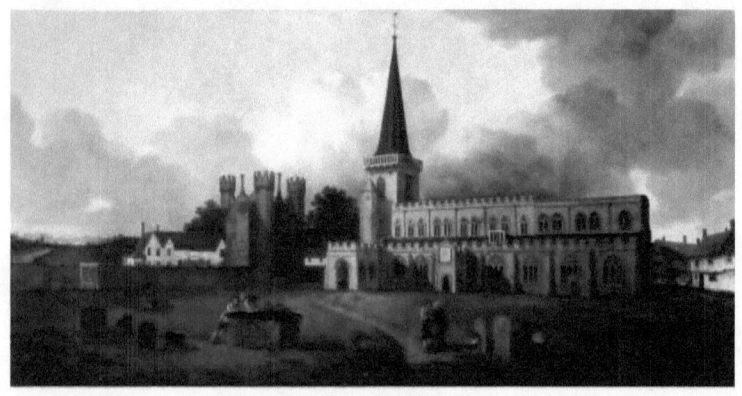

St. Mary's Church Hadleigh, 1750, oil on canvas

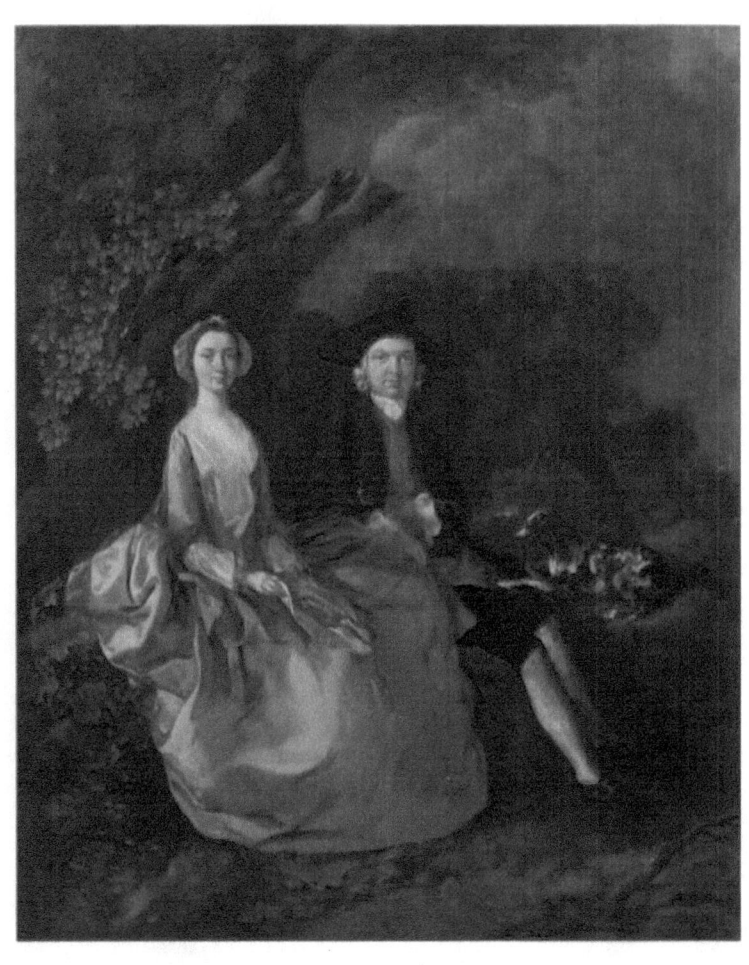

Portrait of Sarah Kirby (née Bull) and John Joshua
Kirby, 1752, oil on canvas

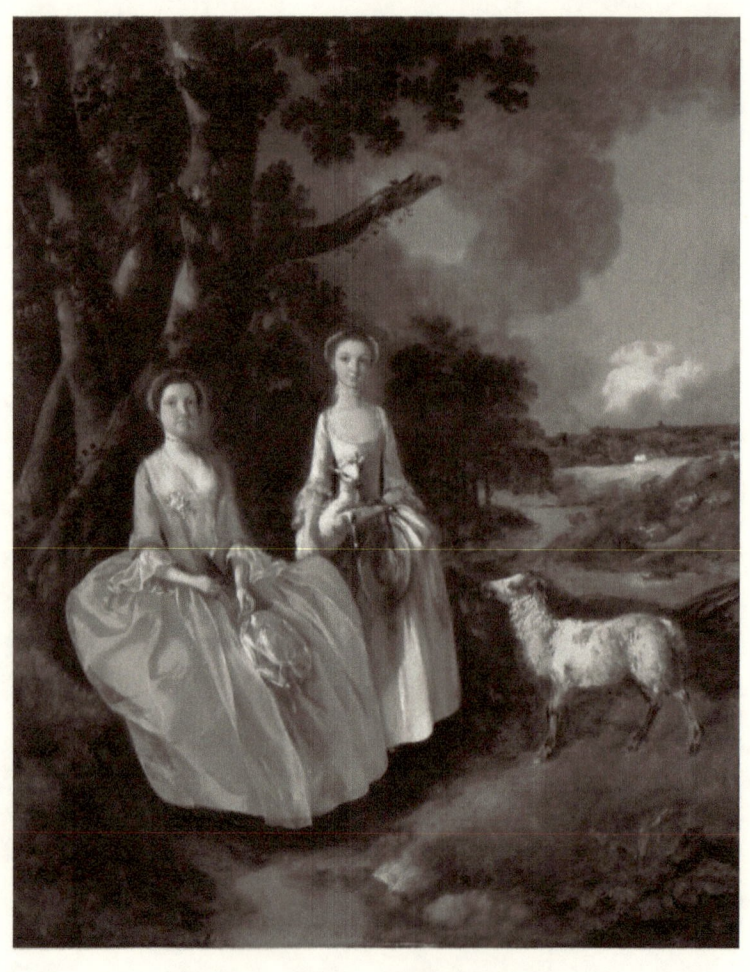

Mrs Mary Cobbold with Her Daughter Anne, 1752, oil
on canvas

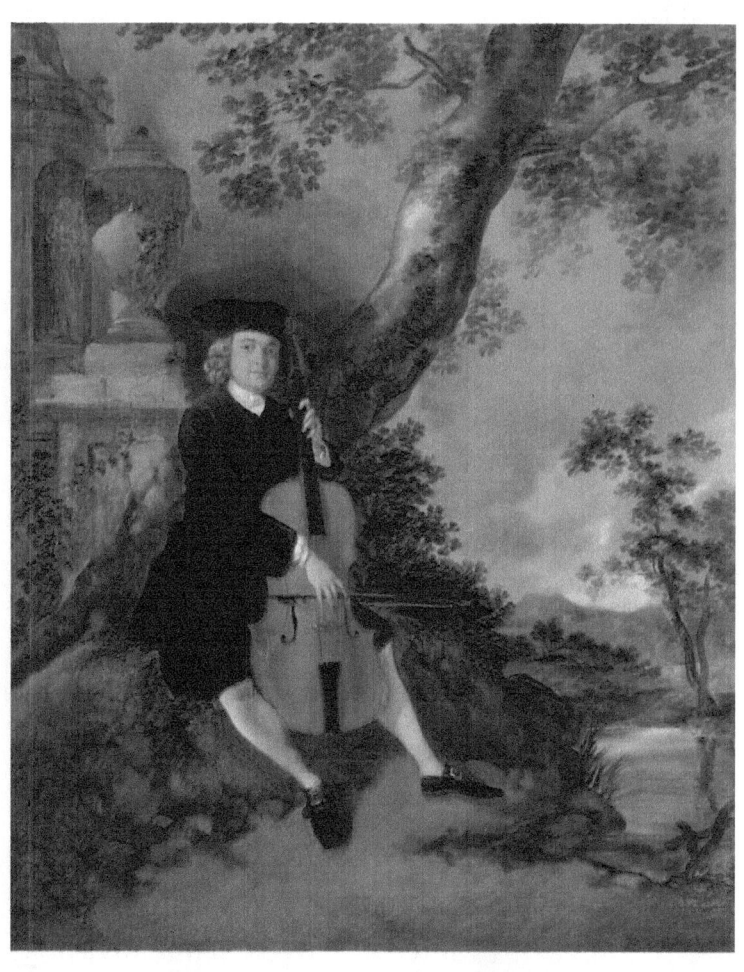

The Rev. John Chafy Playing the Violoncello in a
Landscape, 1752, oil on canvas

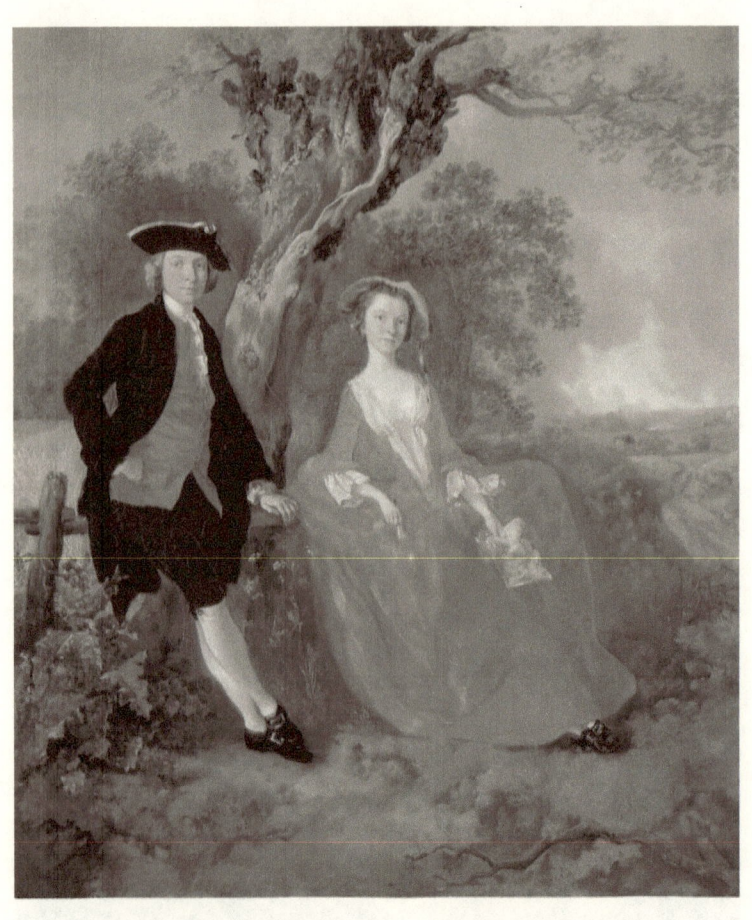

A Couple in a Landscape, 1753, oil on canvas

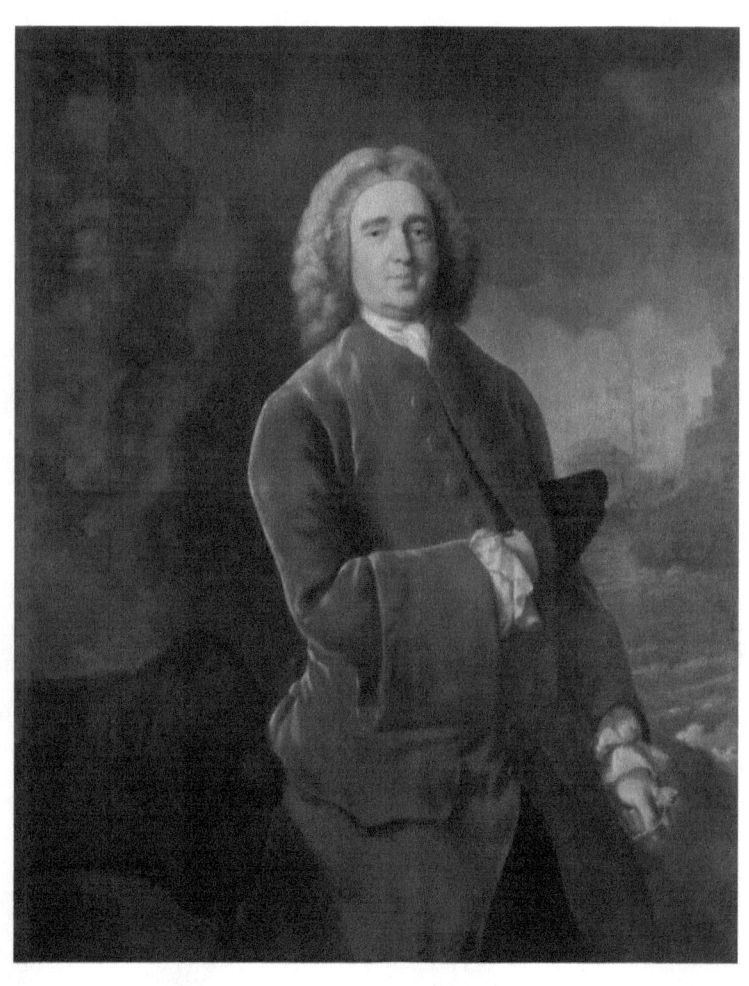

Edward Vernon, 1753, oil on canvas

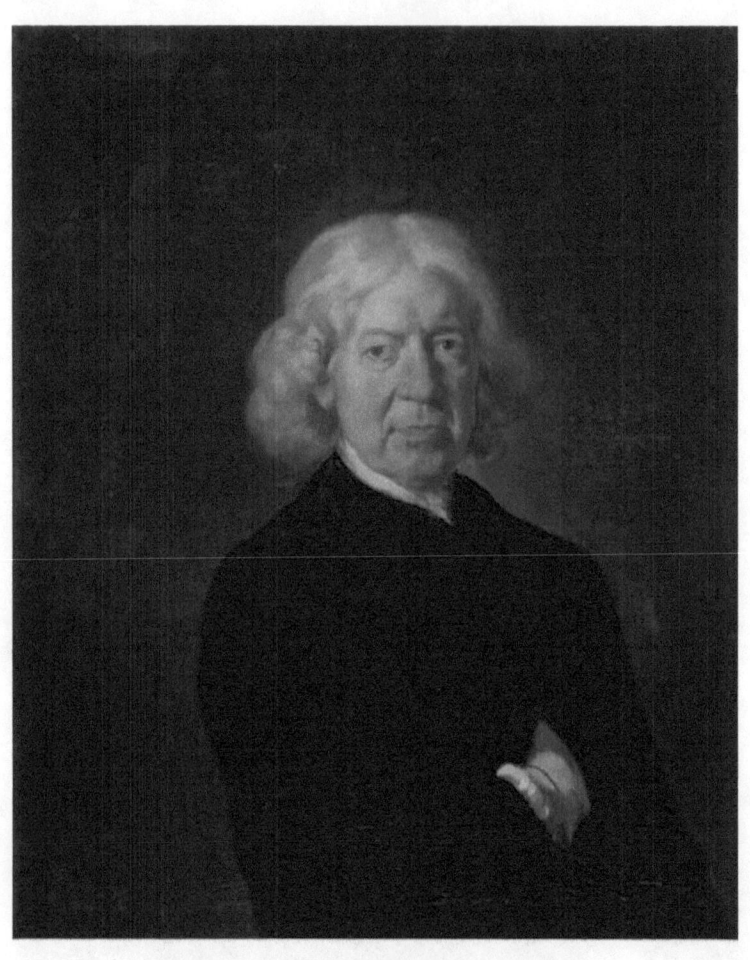

John Kirby, 1753, oil on canvas

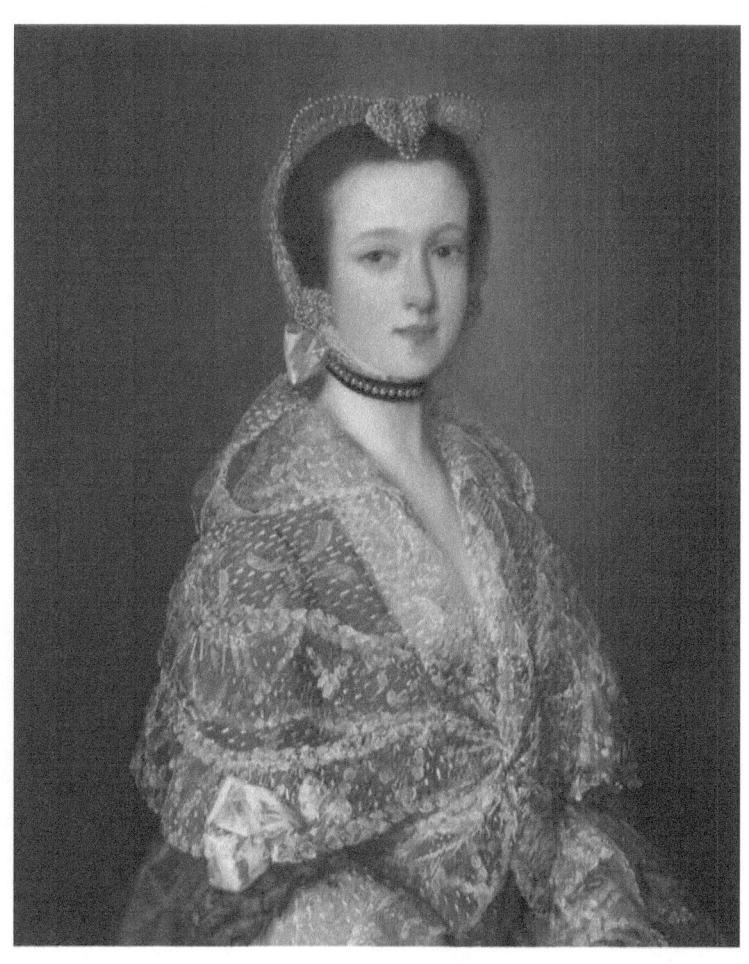

Louisa Barbarina Mansel, Lady Vernon, 1753, oil on canvas

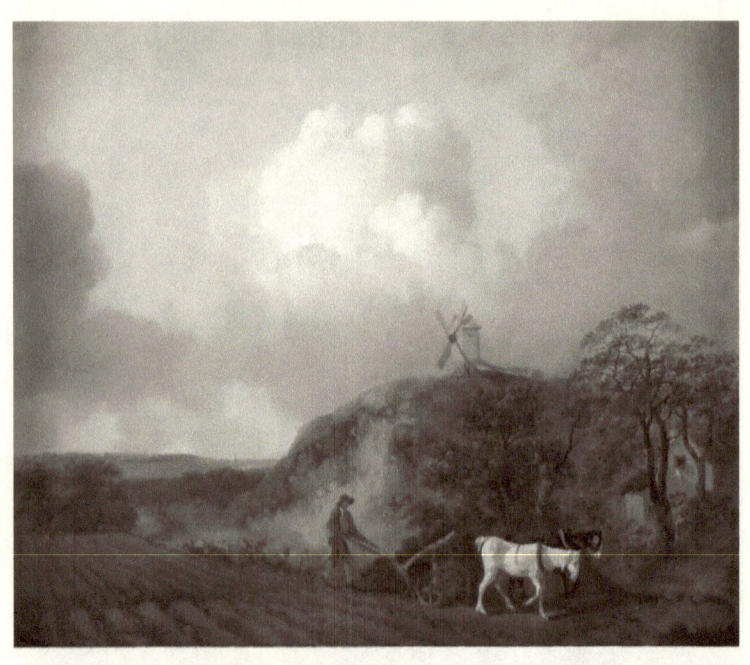

Peasant Ploughing with Two Horses, 1753, oil on canvas

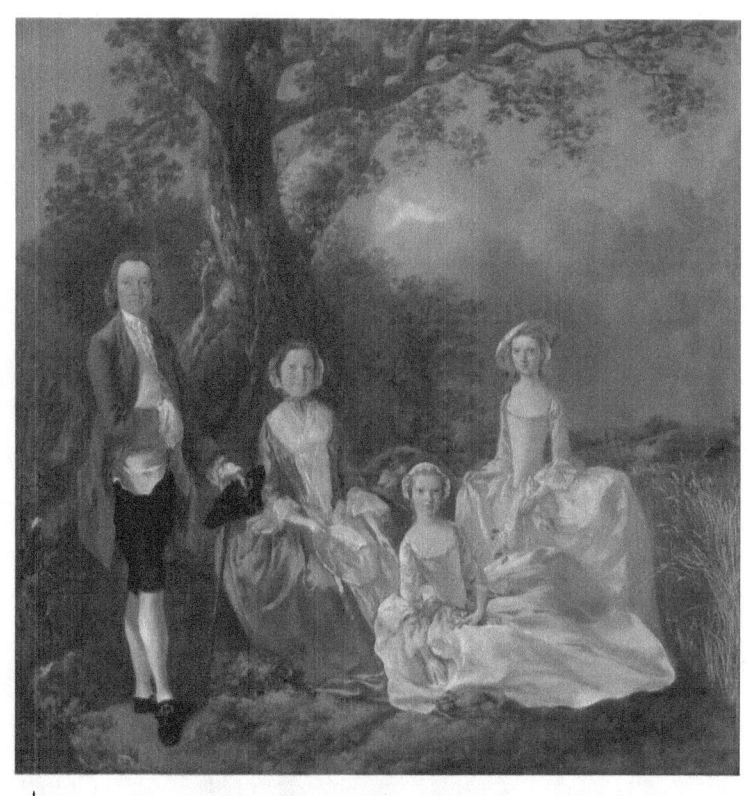

Mr. and Mrs. John Gravenor and their Daughters,
Elizabeth and Ann, 1754, oil on canvas

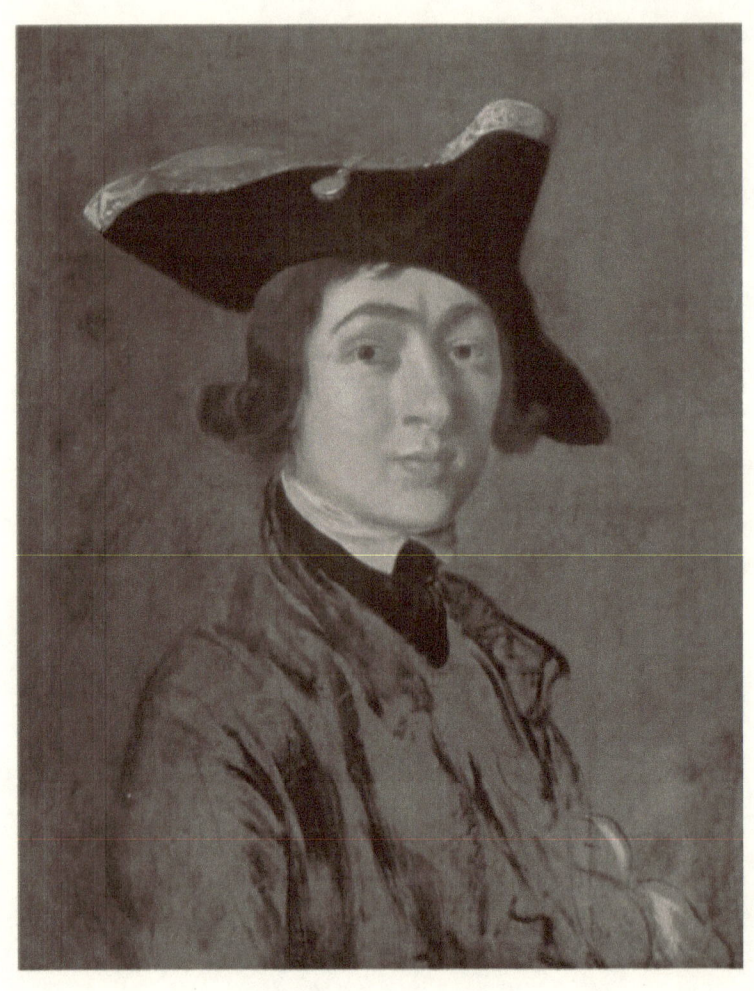

Self portrait, 1754, oil on canvas

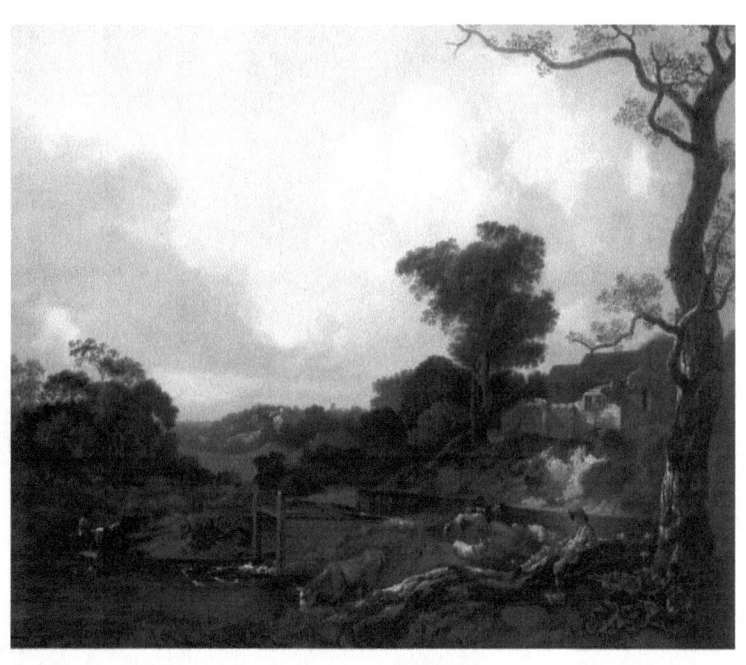

Landscape with a Peasant Reclining by a Weir, 1754, oil on canvas

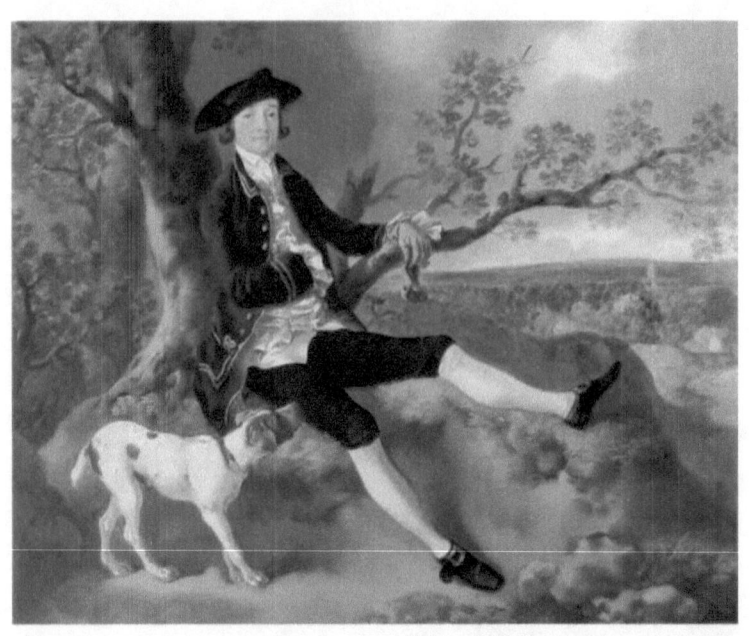

John Plampin, 1755, oil on canvas

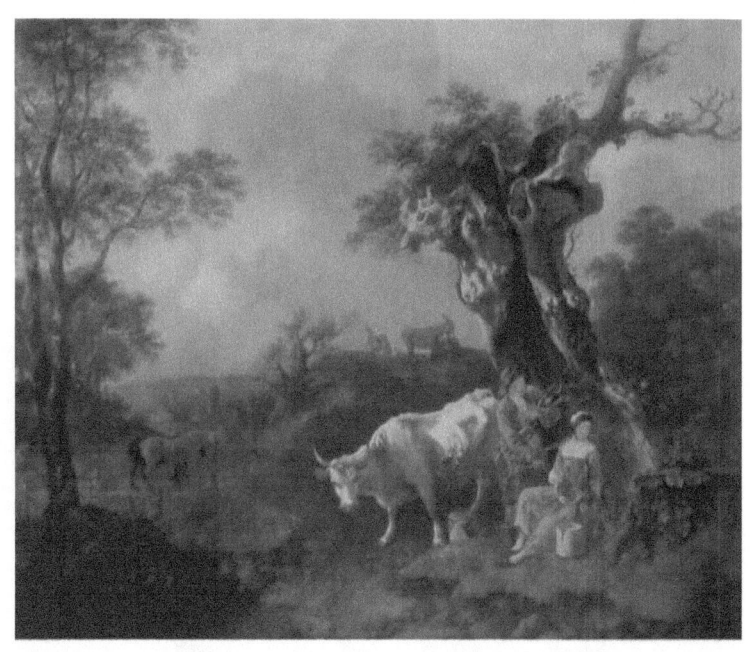

Landscape with a Woodcutter and Milkmaid, 1755, oil on canvas

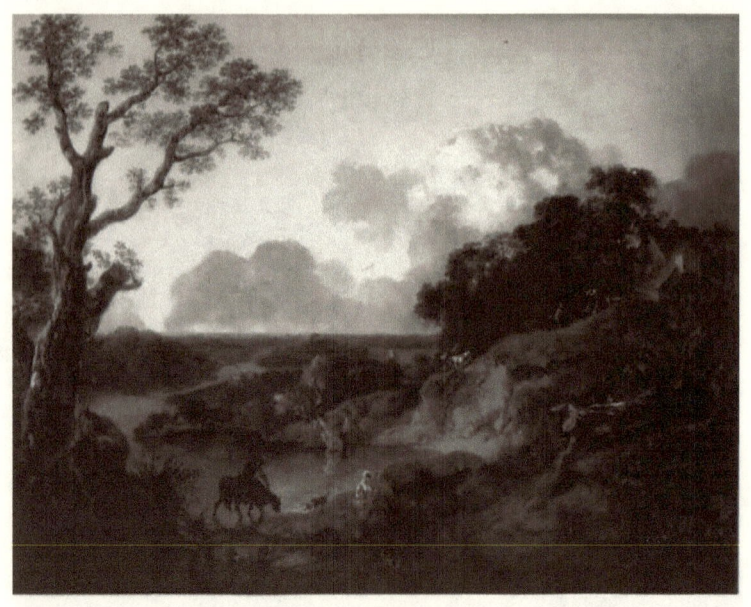

River Landscape with Rustic Lovers, c.1754–c.1756, oil

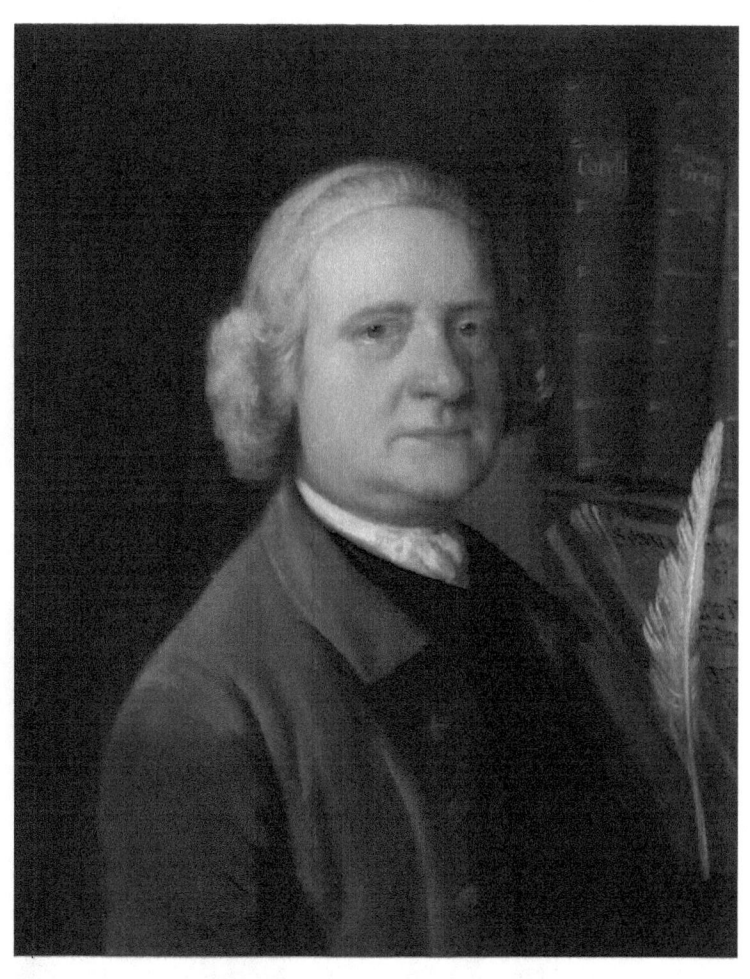

Joseph Gibbs, 1755, oil on canvas

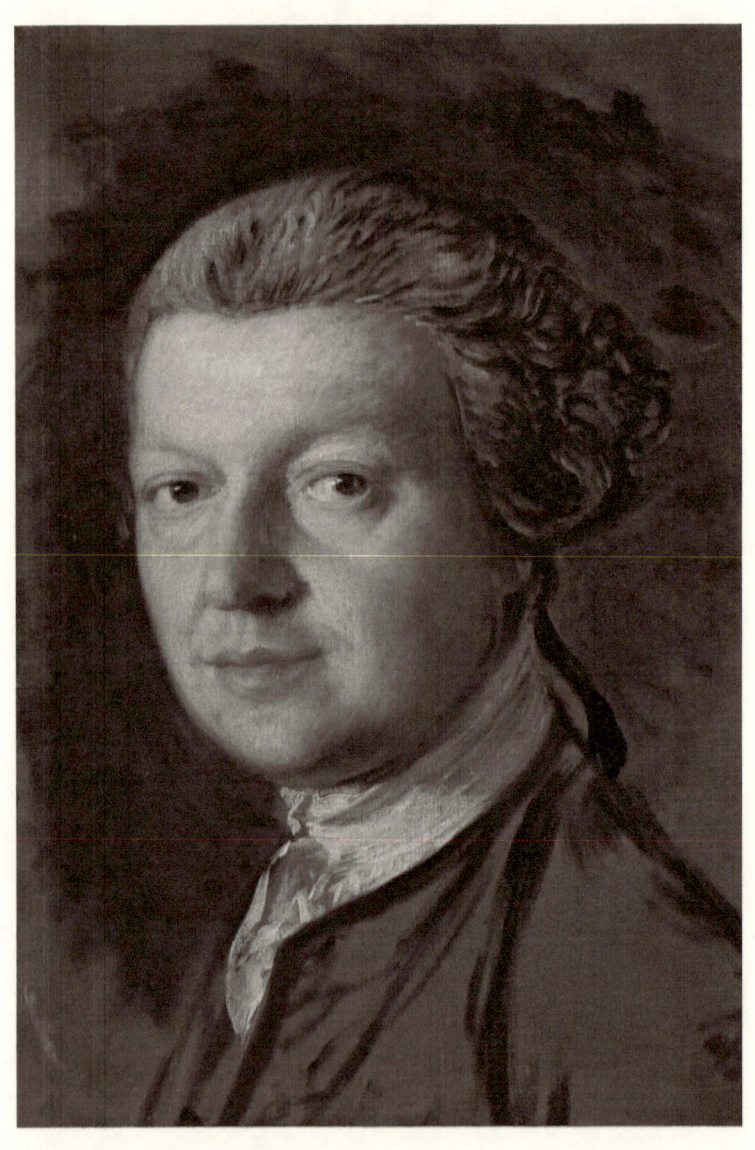

John Joshua Kirby, 1755, oil on canvas

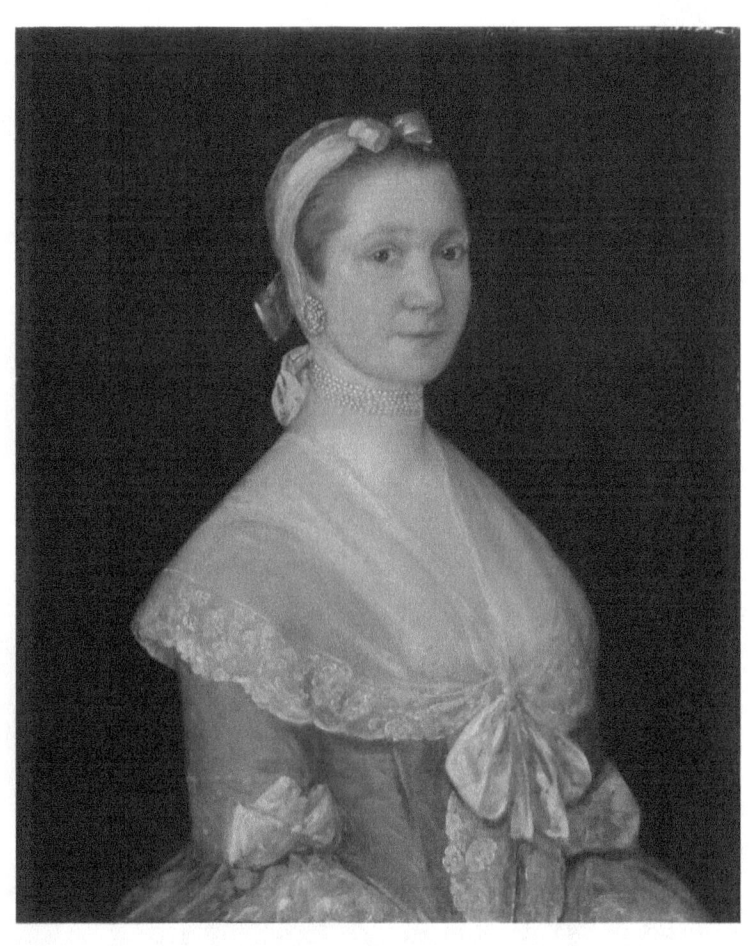

Mrs Prudence Rix, 1756, oil on canvas

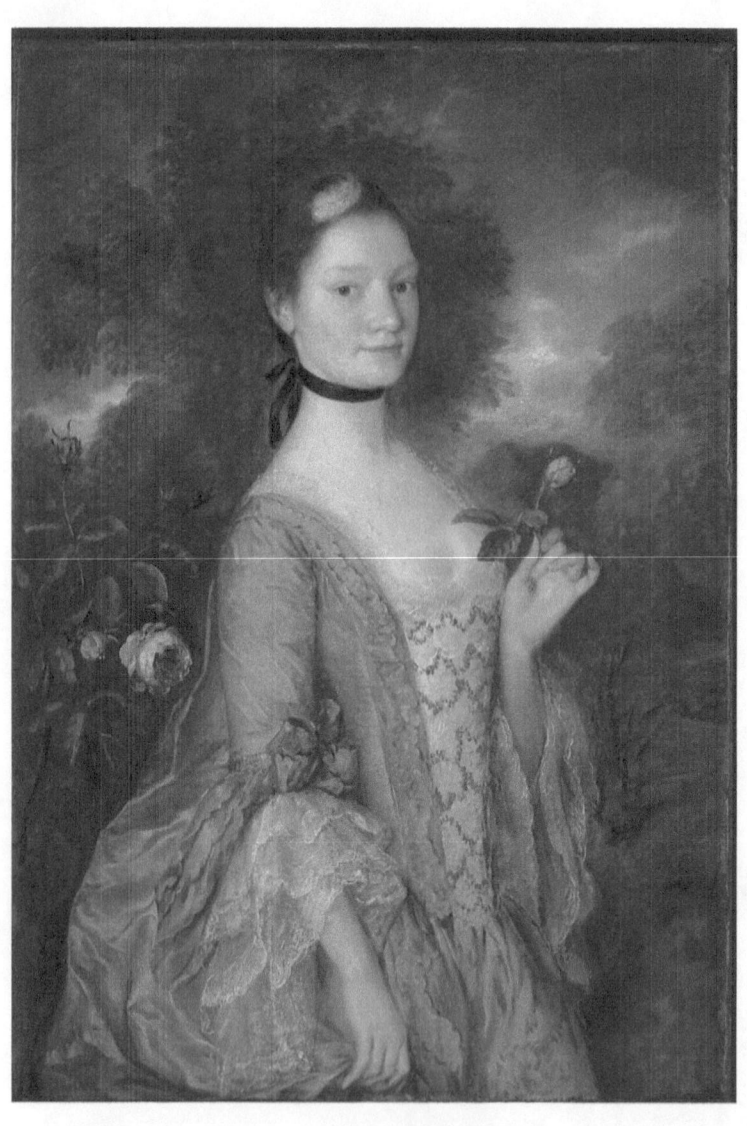

Portrait of Sarah, Lady Innes, 1757, oil on canvas

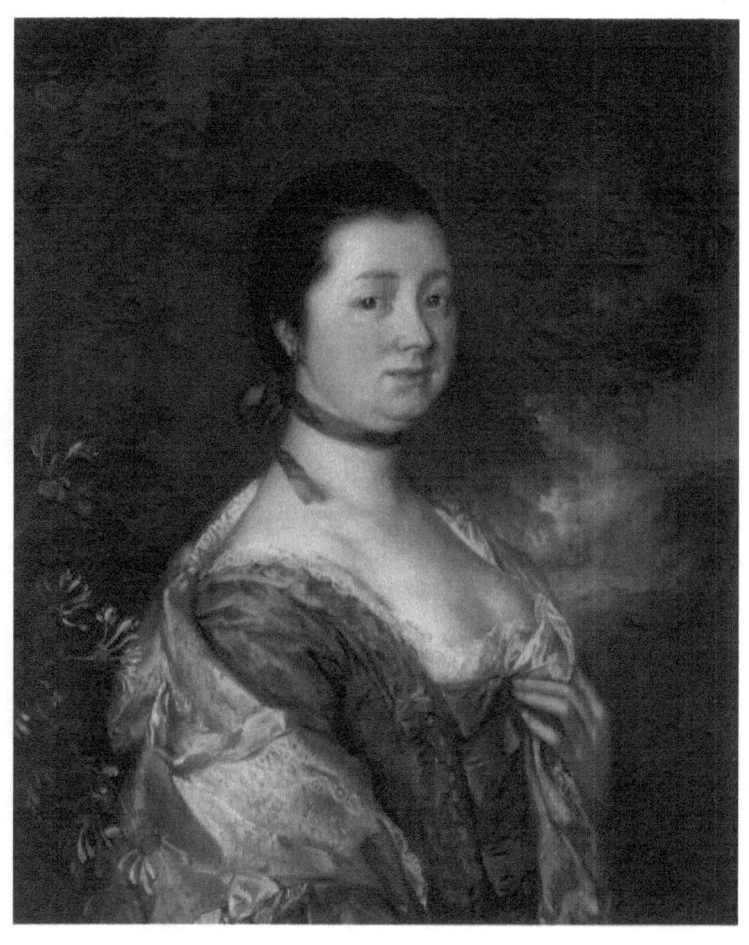

The Artist's Wife, 1758, oil on canvas

Gainsborough's wife, the former Margaret Burr (1728-1798) may have been the illegitimate daughter of the duke of Bedford. Gainsborough's early portraits are fresh and delicate, often in the contemporary French manner with a touch of van Dyck.

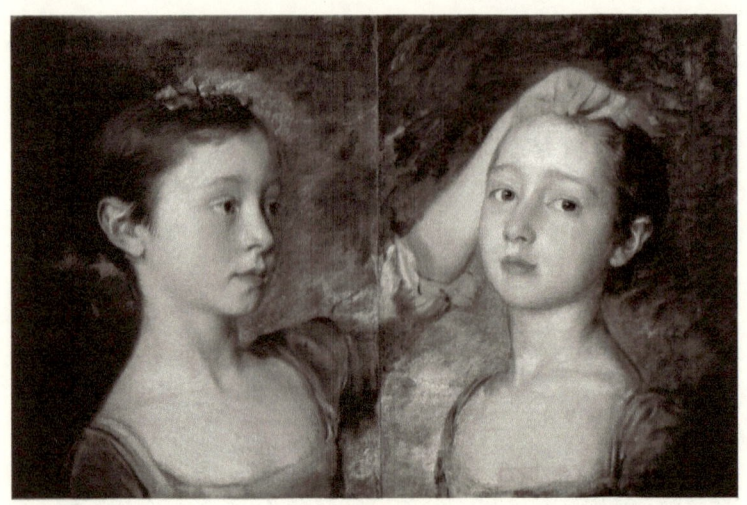

Portrait of the Painter's Two Daughters, 1758, oil on canvas

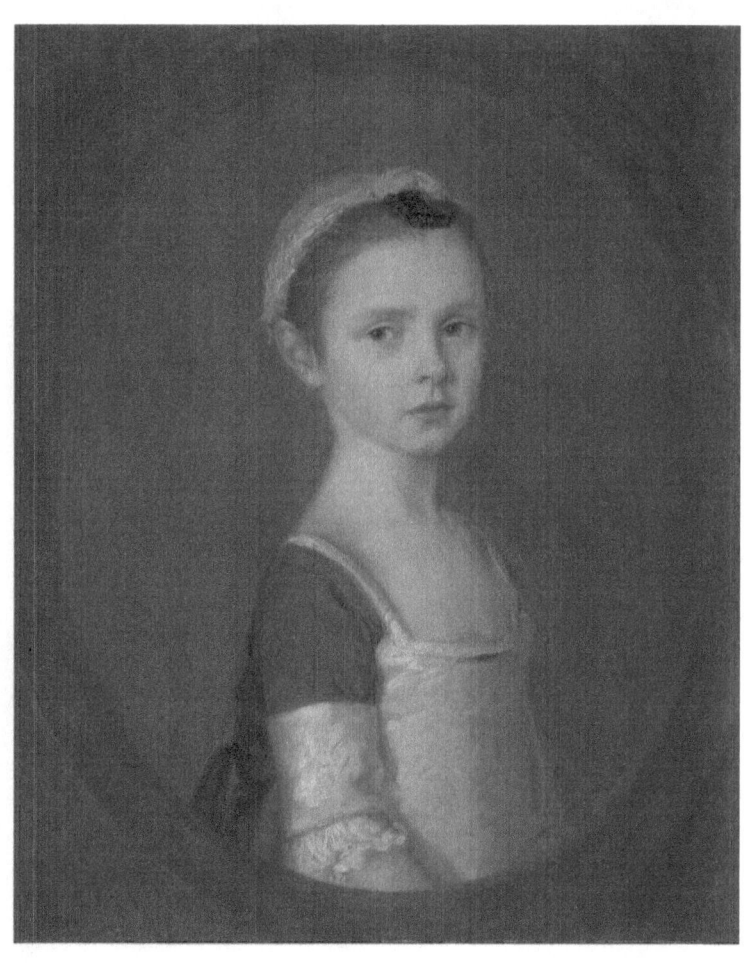

Miss Susanna Gardiner, 1758, oil on canvas

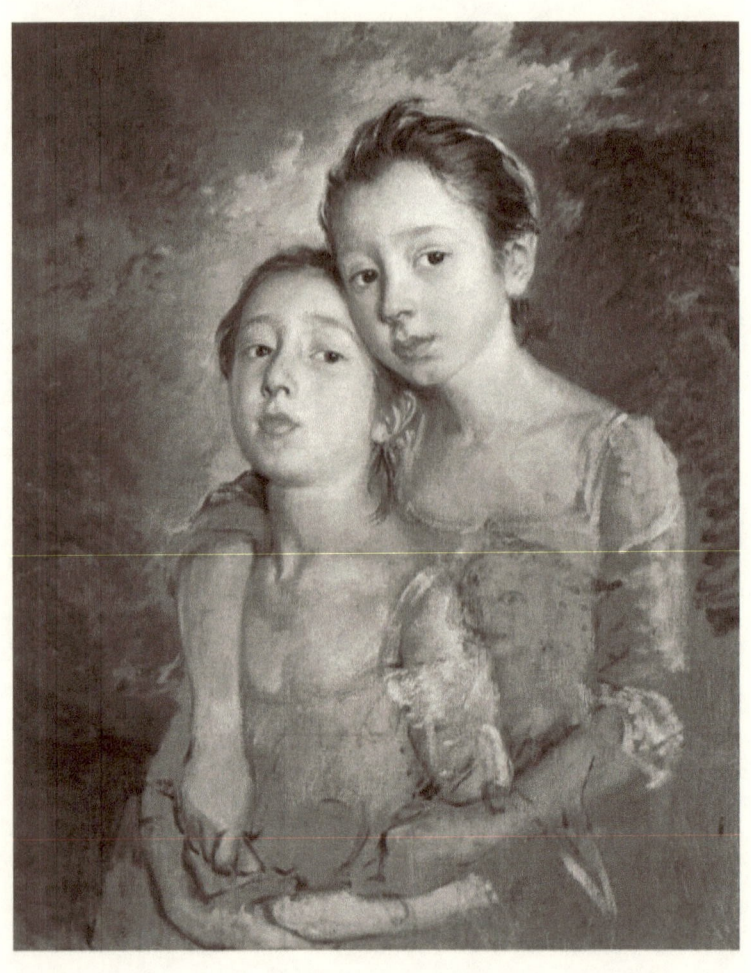

Portrait of the artist's daughter with a cat (unfinished),
1759, oil on canvas

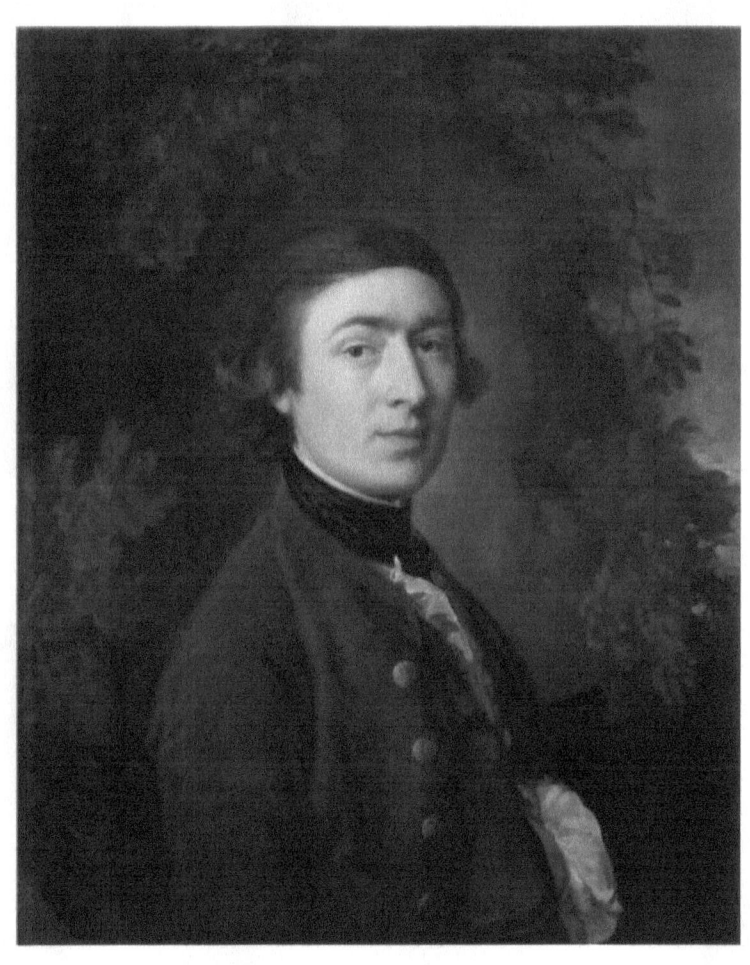

Self portrait, 1759, oil on canvas

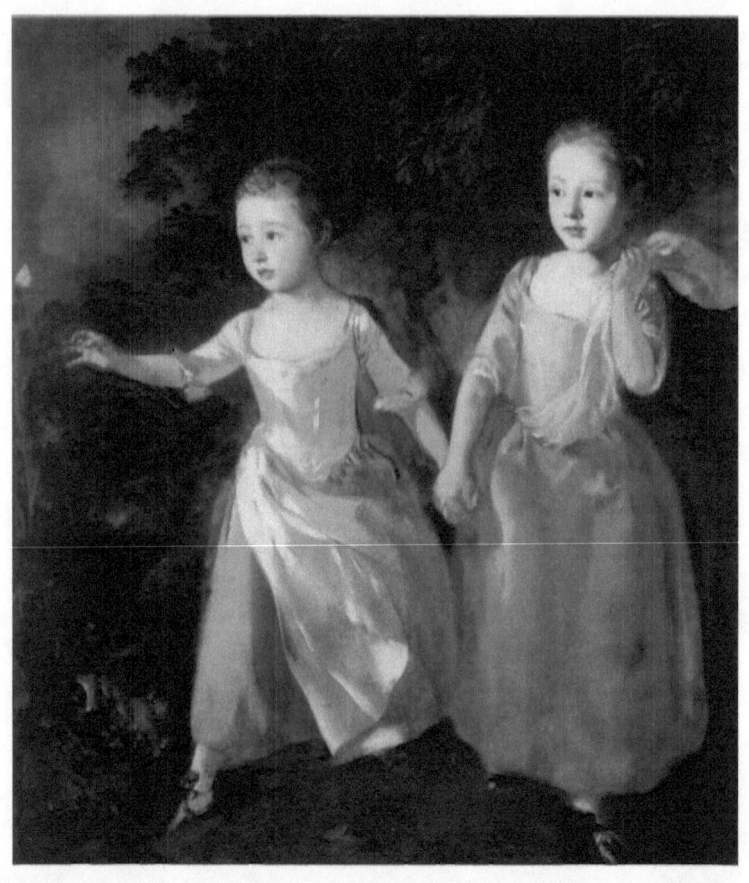

The Painter's Daughters chasing a Butterfly, 1759, oil on canvas

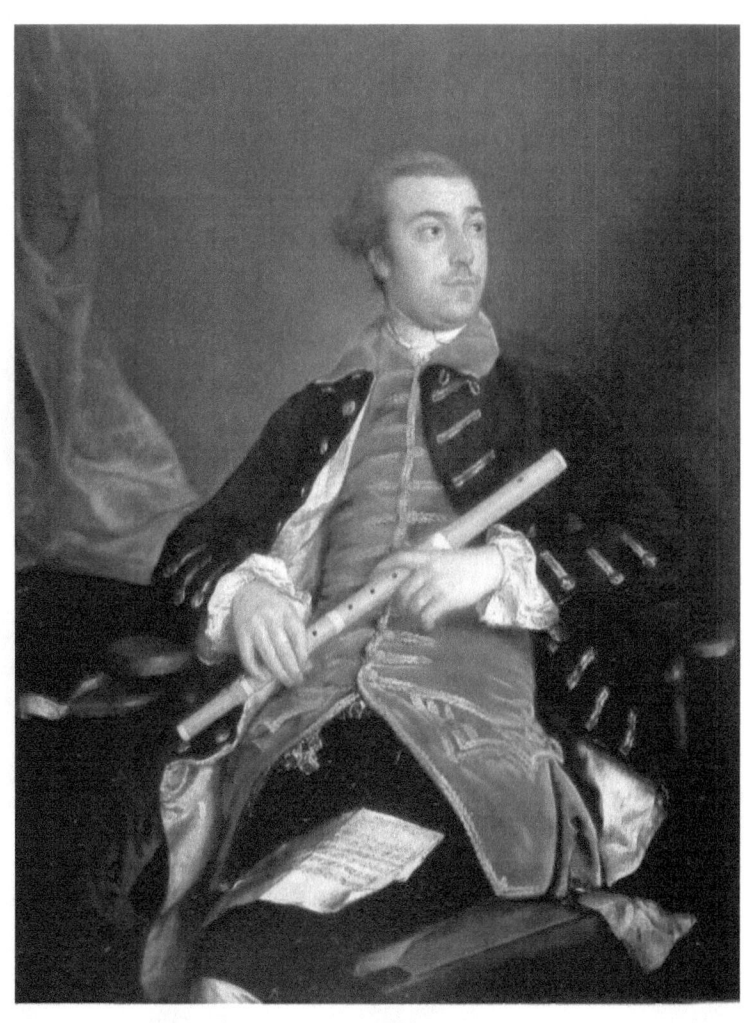

William Wollaston, 1759, oil on canvas

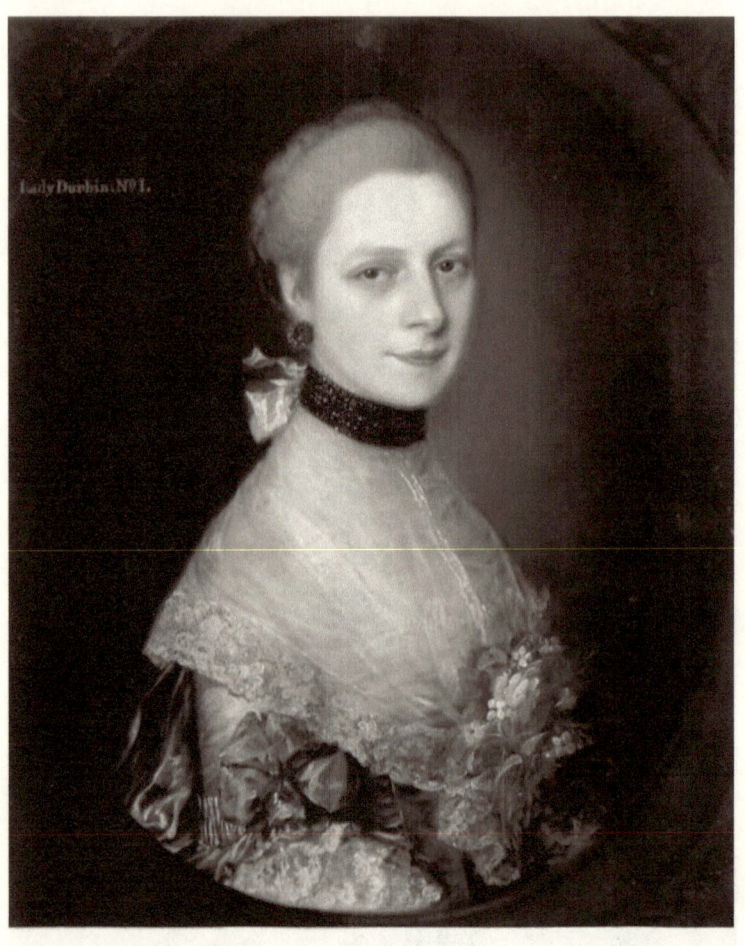

Mrs John Durbin, née Elizabeth Collett, 1759, oil on canvas

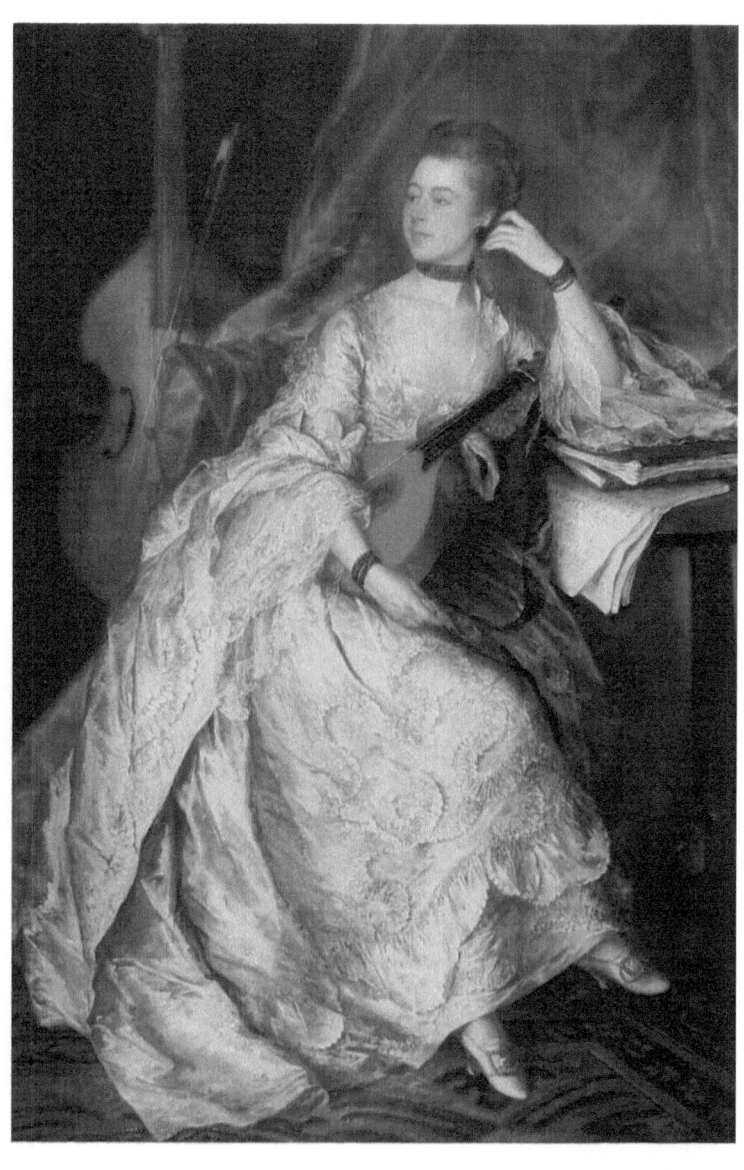

Portrait of Ann Ford (later Mrs. Thicknesse), 1760, oil
on canvas

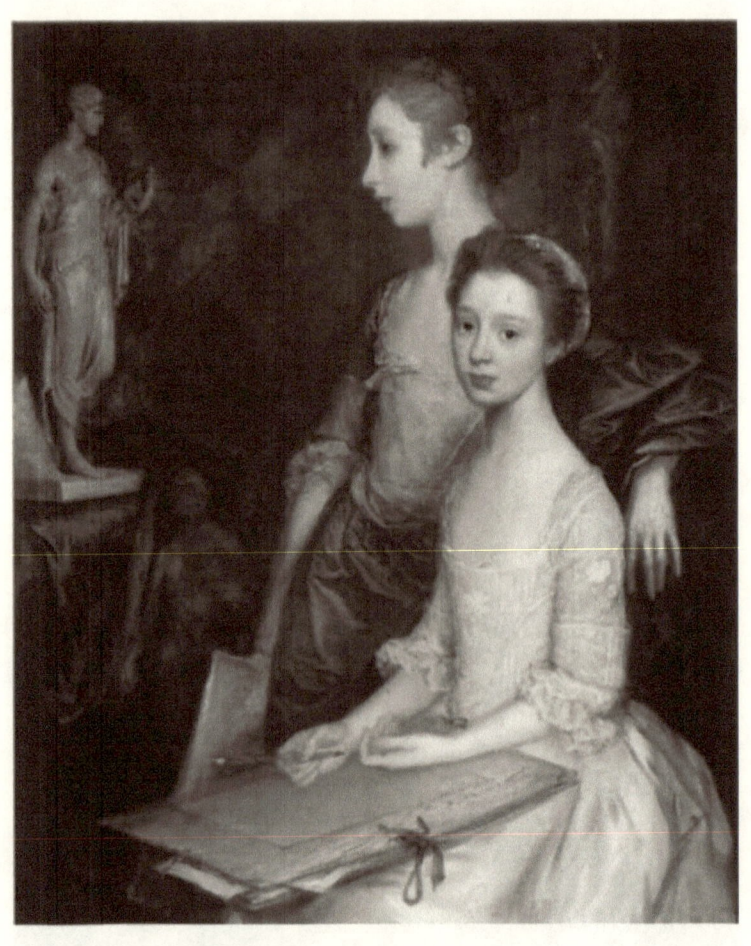

Portrait of the Molly and Peggy, 1760, oil on canvas

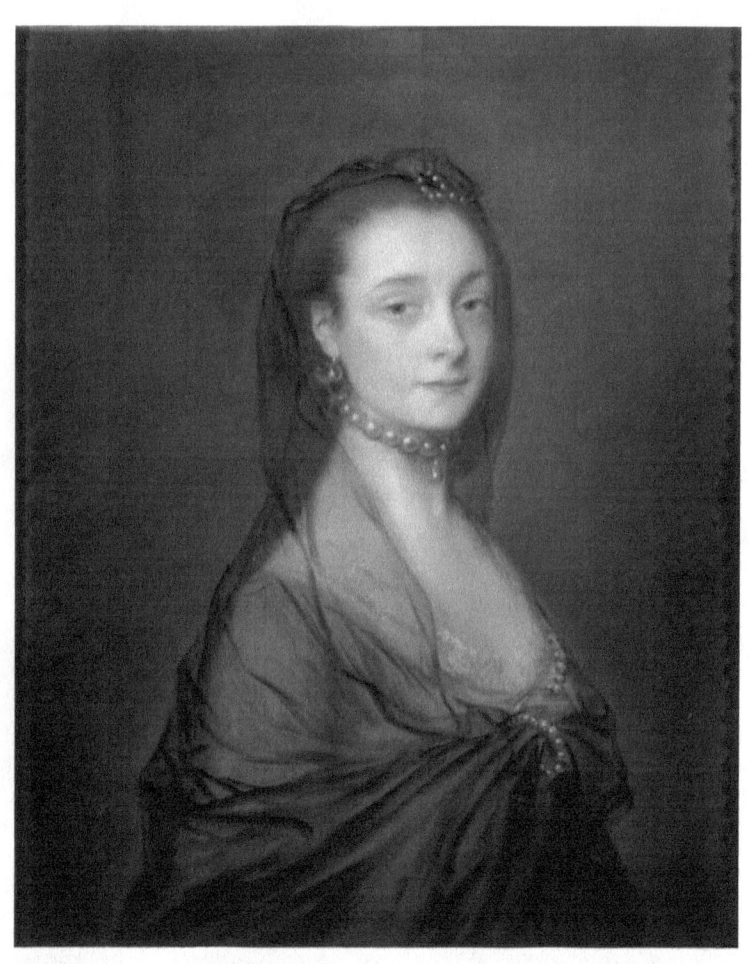

Elizabeth Cowper, 1760, oil on canvas

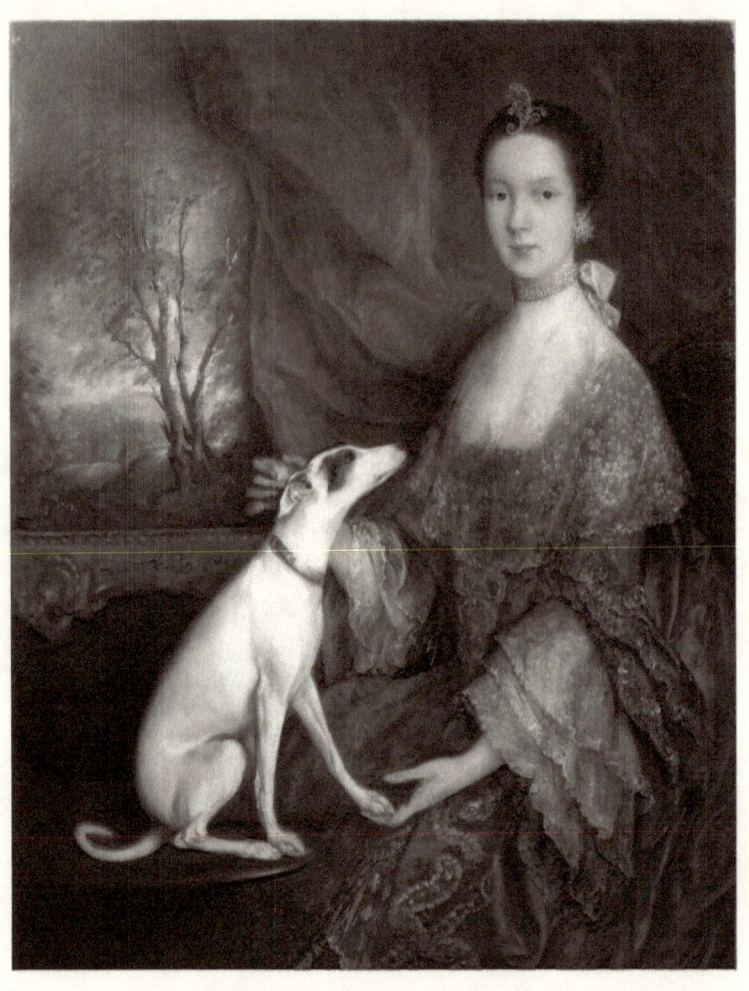

Portrait of Elizabeth Jackson, Mrs Morton Pleydell,
1760, oil on canvas

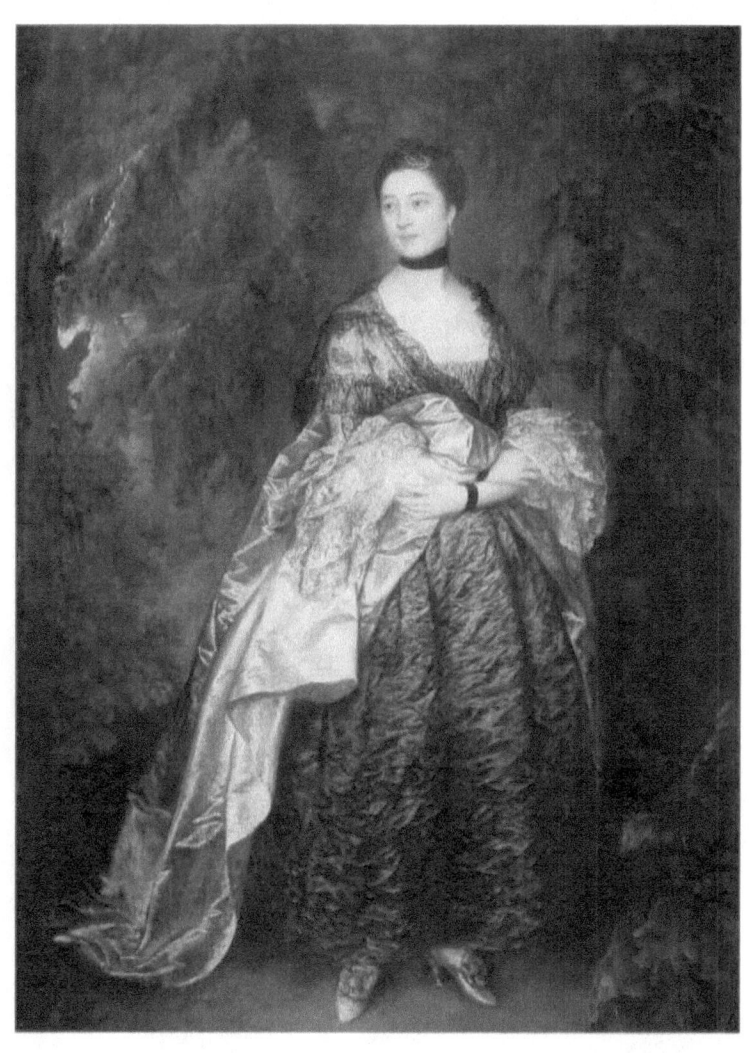

Lady Alston, 1762, oil on canvas

This work dates from Gainsborough's mature period, when he resided in Bath as a fashionable portraitist of the aristocracy. Following the elegant Van Dyck tradition, he places the model in a broad landscape background. However, the strong contrasts of the lighting of the figure and the flashing effect achieved on the silk of her dress against the deep, impenetrable forest behind her make this mysterious and poetic portrait a completely original work.

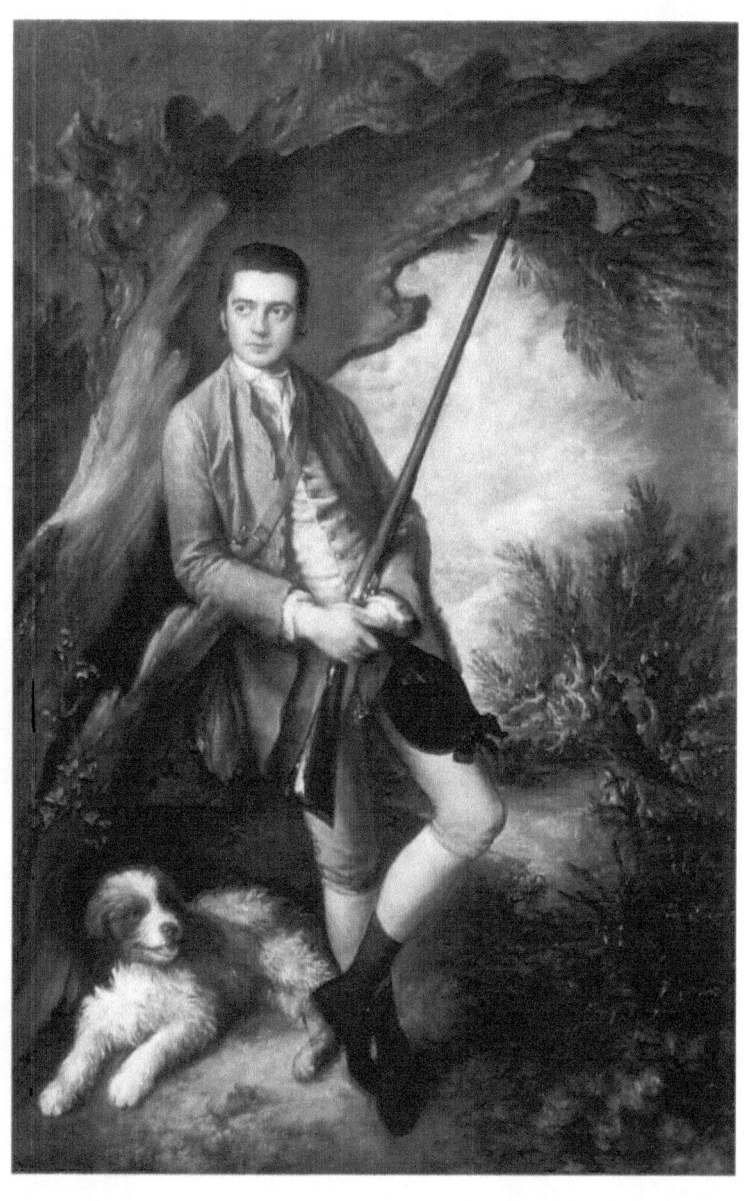

William Poyntz of Midgham and his Dog Amber, 1762,
oil on canvas

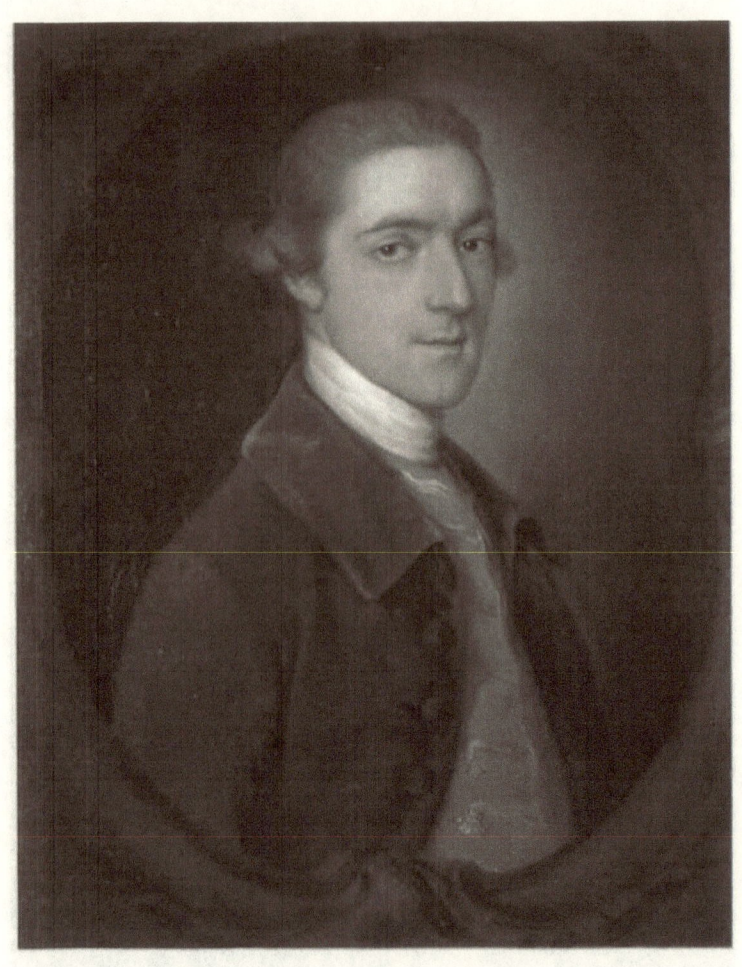

John Spencer, 1st Earl Spencer, 1763, oil on canvas

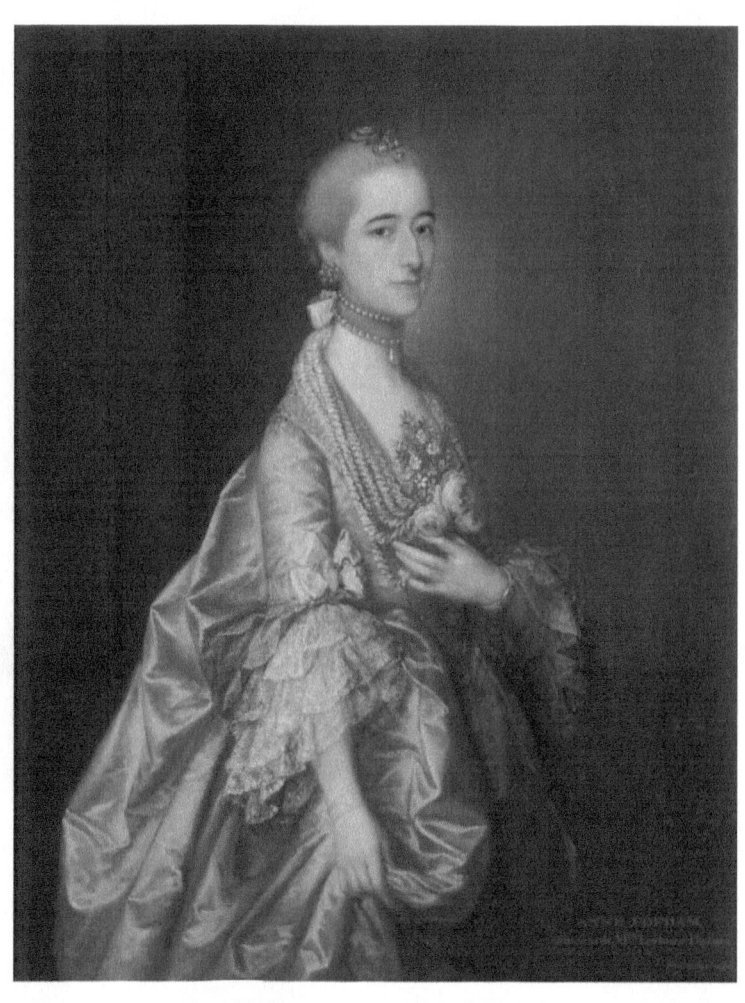

Ann Leyborne, 1763, oil on canvas

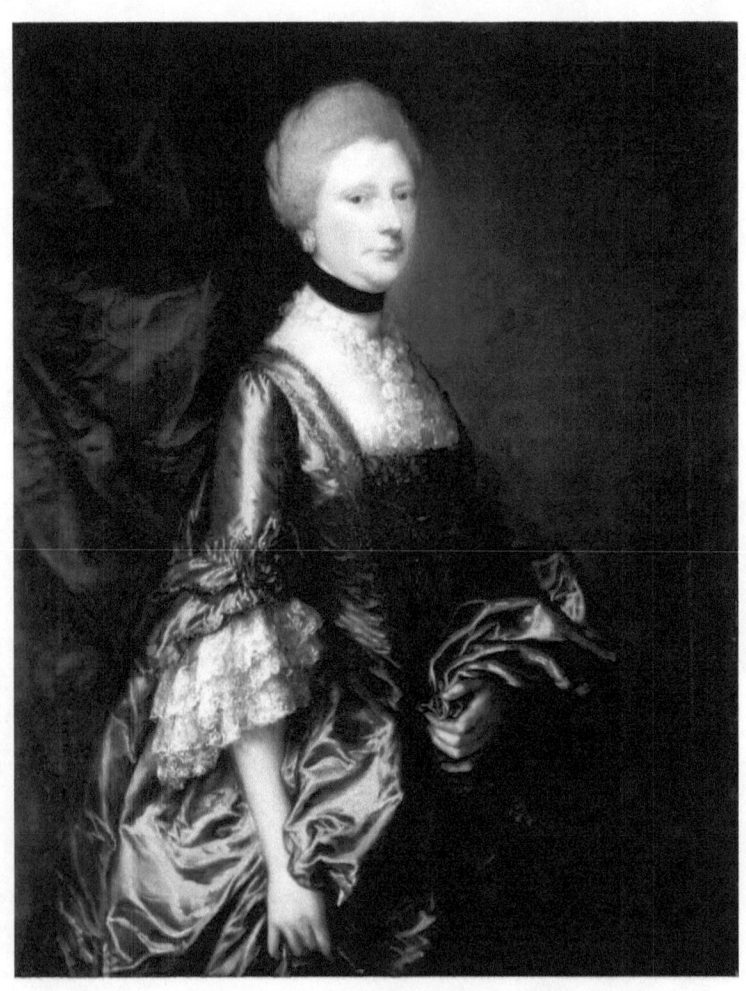

Harriet, Viscountess Tracy, 1763, oil on canvas

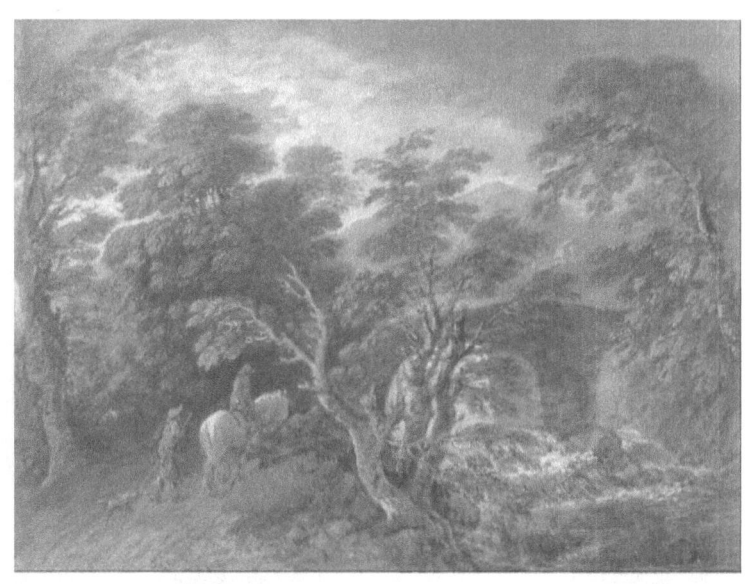

Hilly Landscape with Figures Approaching a Bridge,
1763, watercolor

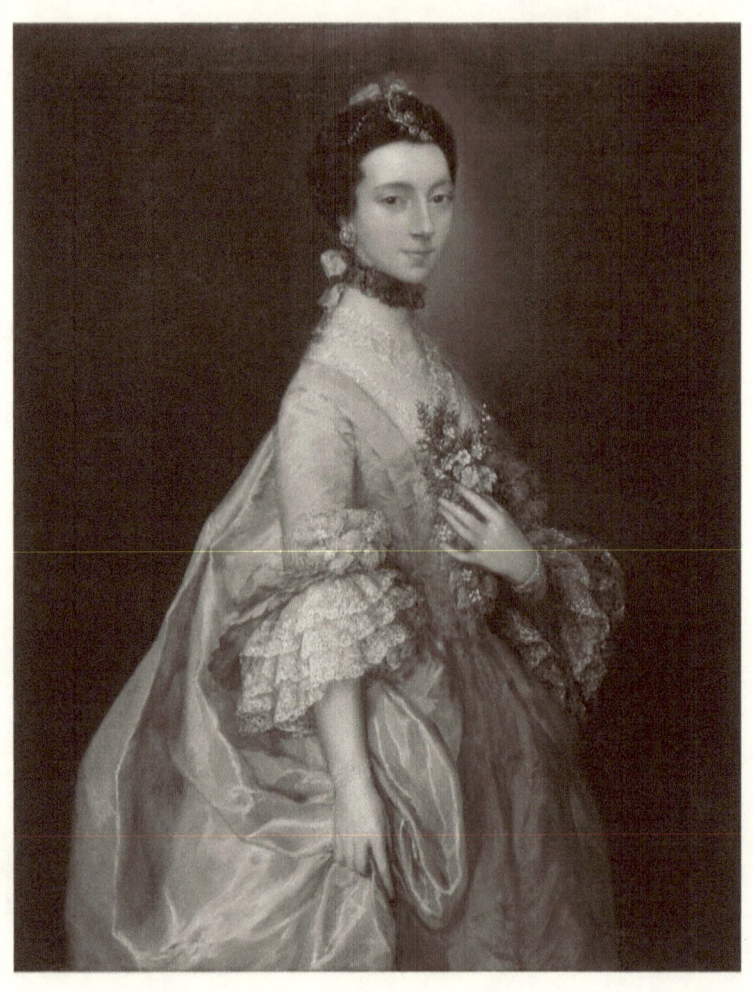

Mary Little, Later Lady Carr, 1763, oil on canvas

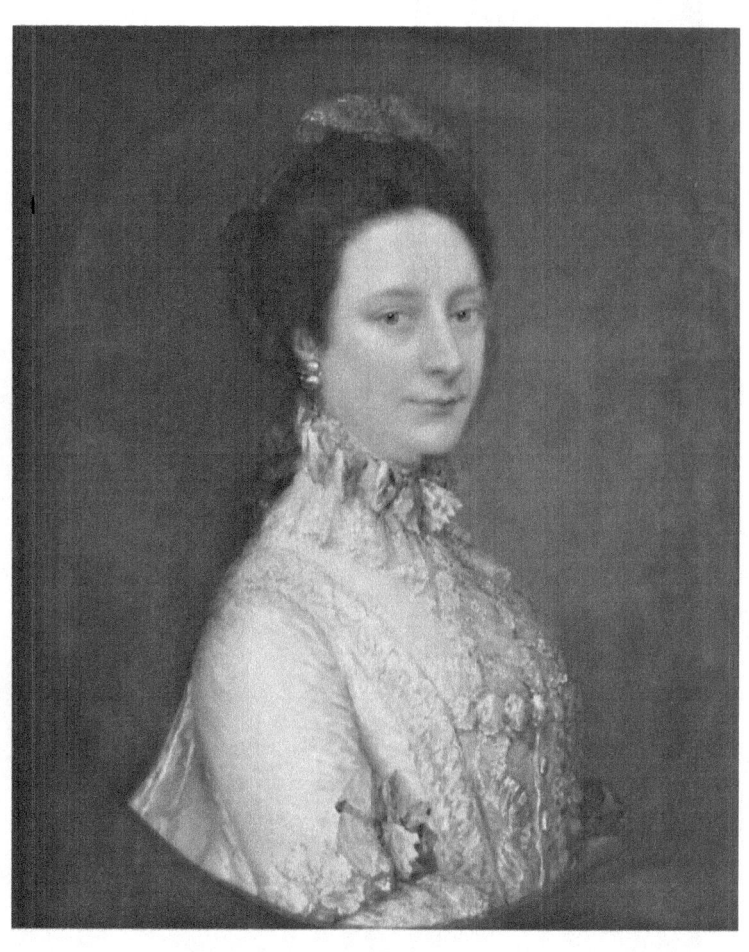

Mrs Charlotte Frere, 1763, oil on canvas

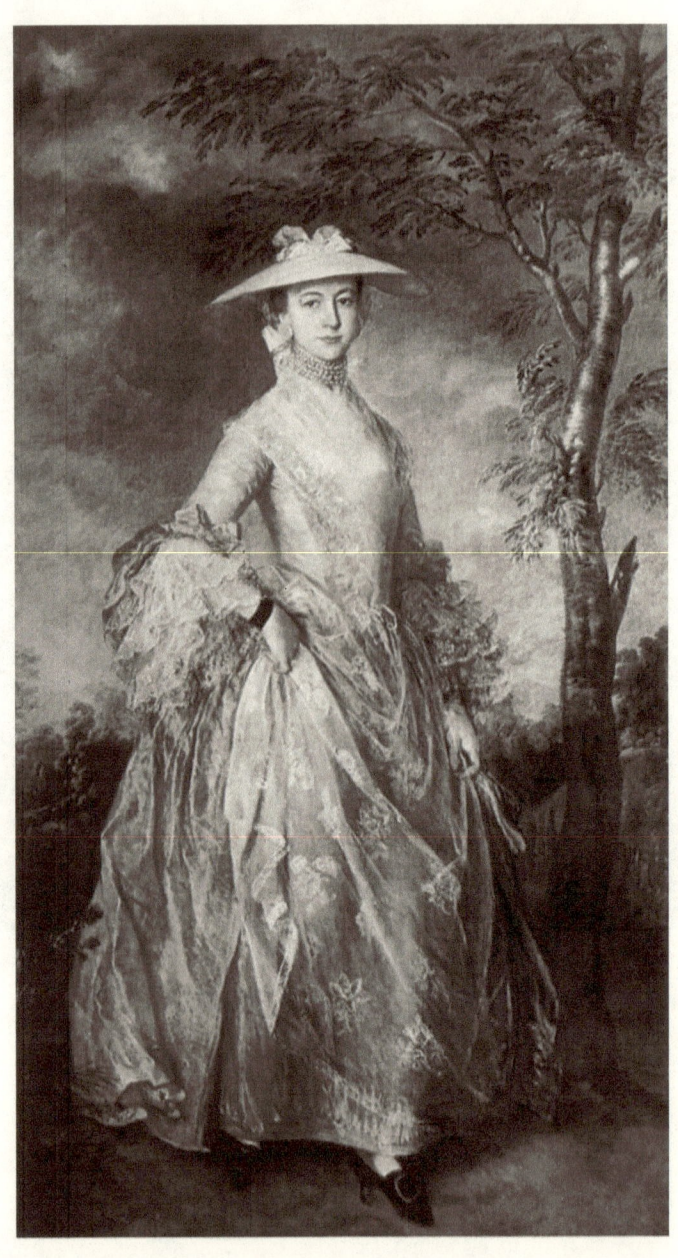

Mary, Countess of Howe, 1764, Oil on canvas

Together with Joshua Reynolds, Thomas Gainsborough was one of the artists who carried English landscape painting to its greatest heights in the 18th century. Portaiture and landscape were the two most important genres in 18th-century English art and became a symbol of national identity. Gainsborough worked in both genres with great success owing to the quality of his work. Indeed, he combined the two genres by using landscape backgrounds for his portraits.

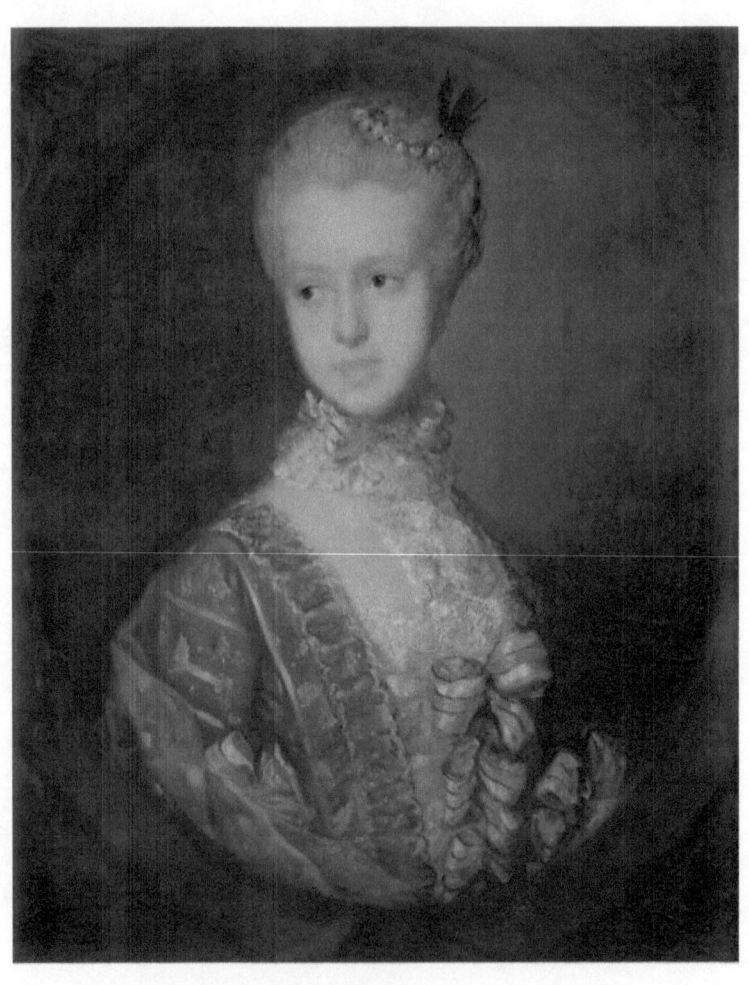

Elizabeth Wrottesly, 1764-65, oil on canvas,

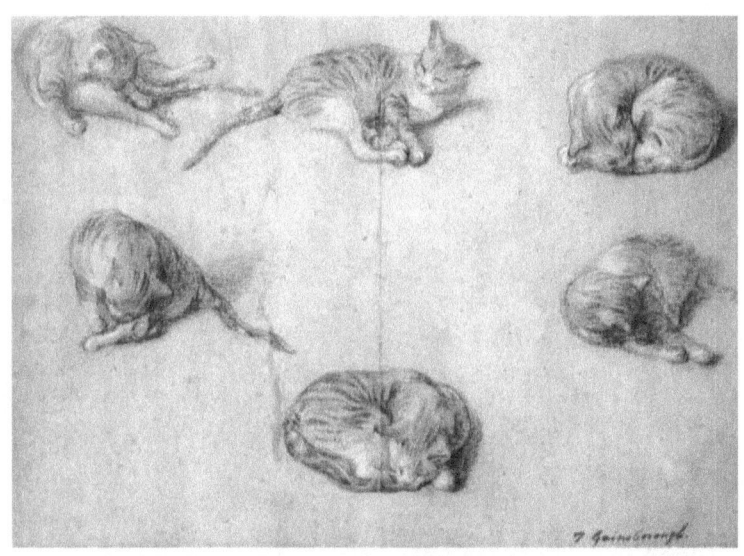

Six studies of a cat, 1765-70, Black and white chalk on grey paper

A cat in typically feline poses: alert, half-asleep, curled up snugly, and washing itself at great length. These cats by the English painter Gainsborough are extremely lifelike. This chalk drawing is unusual for him, for he seldom portrayed animals - most of his drawings were of landscapes and people. Tradition has it that the artist produced this drawing as a gift to his hostess while staying at her home. This would seem to be confirmed by the signature, for Gainsborough did not normally sign his drawings.

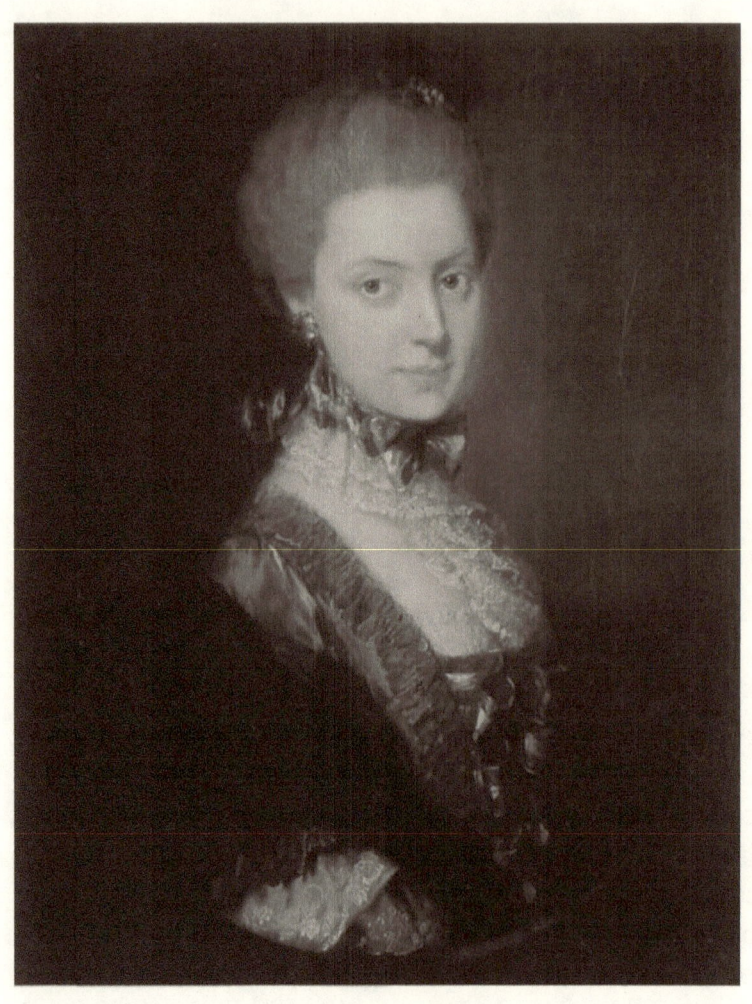

Elizabeth Wrottesley, 1765, oil on canvas

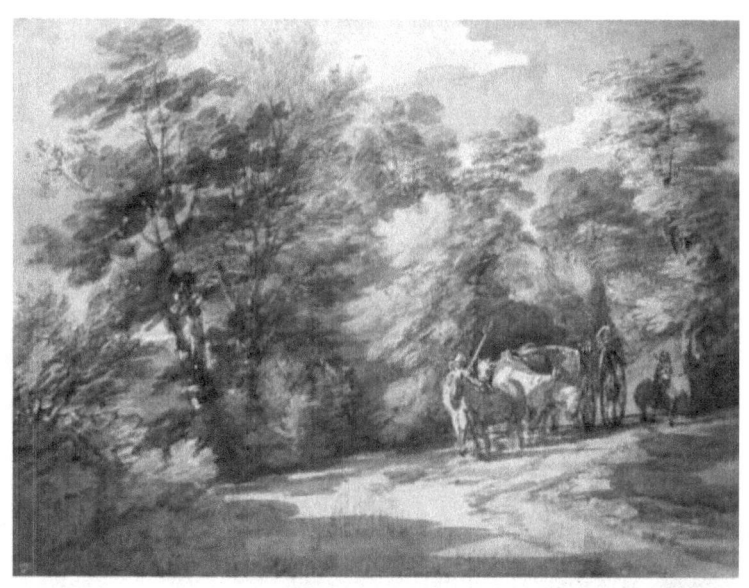

Wooded Landscape with a Waggon in the Shade, 1765,
oil on canvas

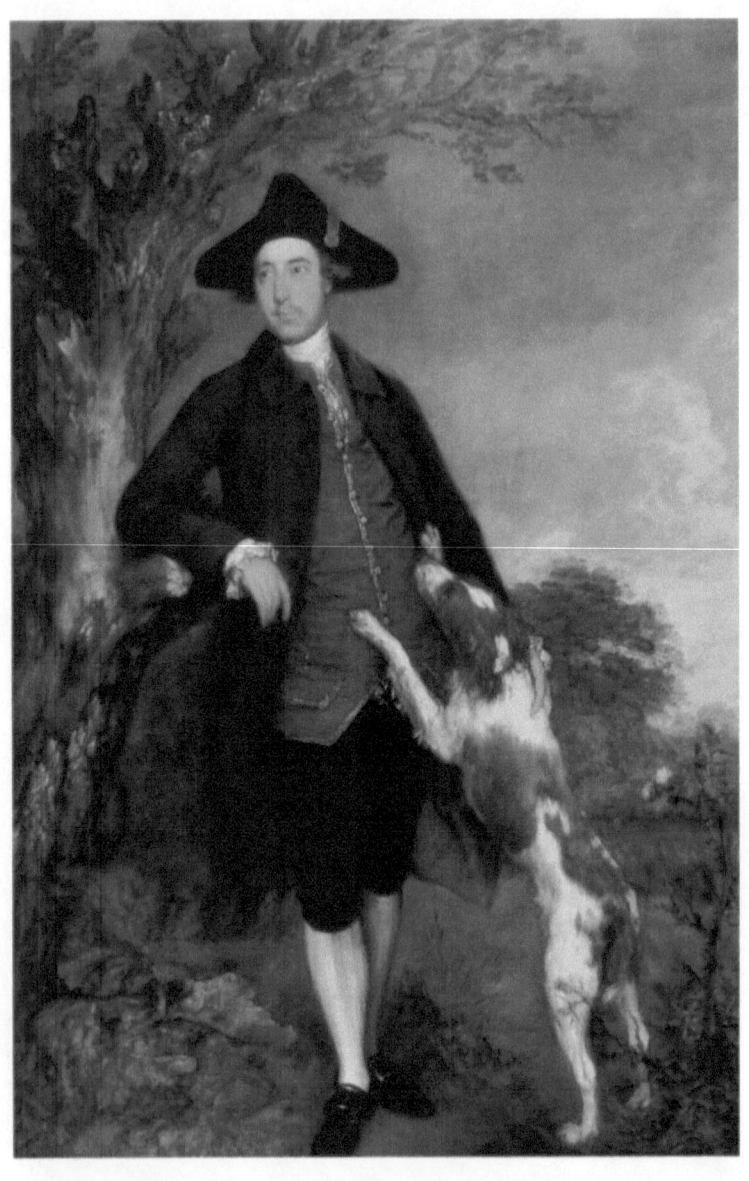

Portrait of George Venables Vernon, 2nd Lord Vernon,
1767, oil on canvas

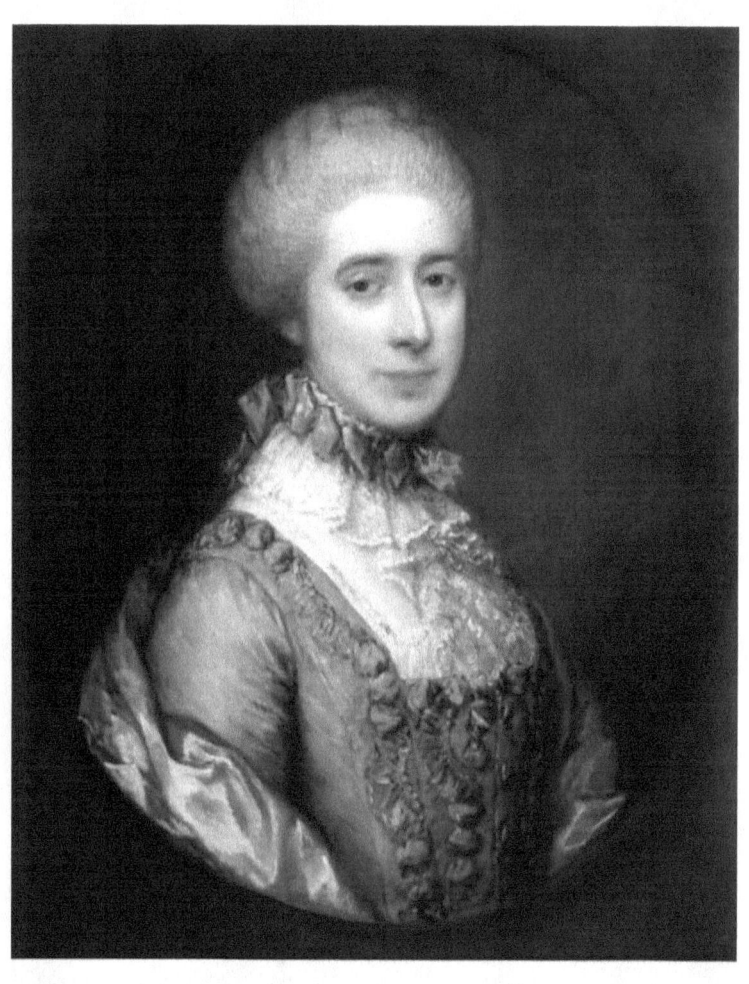

Portrait of Mrs. Awse, 1767, oil on canvas

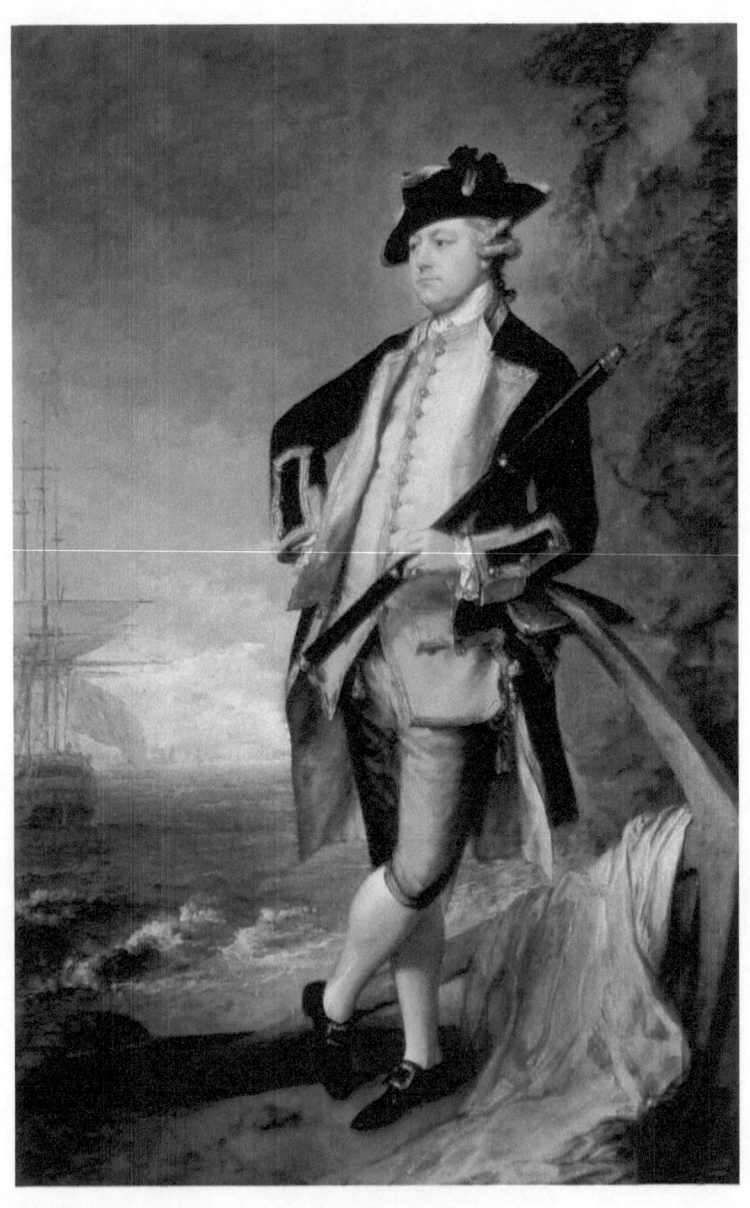

Augustus John, third Earl of Briston, 1768, oil on canvas

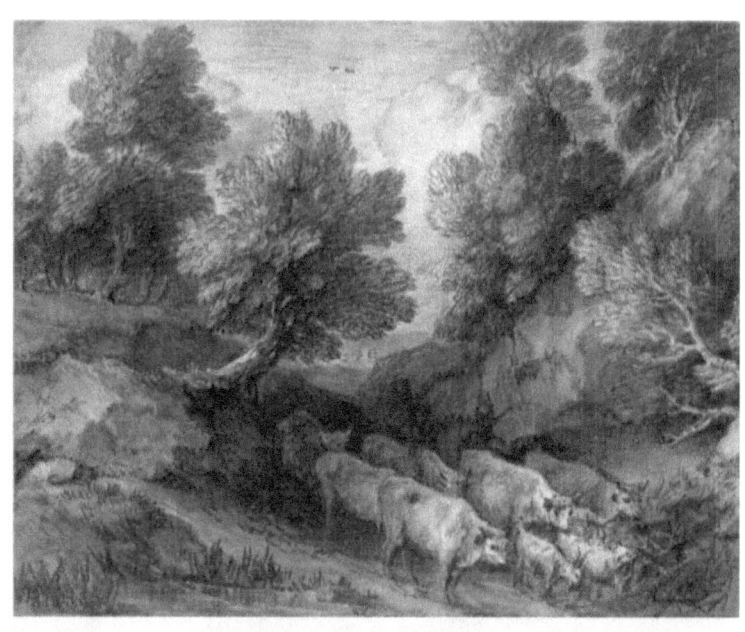

Wooded Landscape with Cattle and Goats, c.1768-
c.1772, chalk

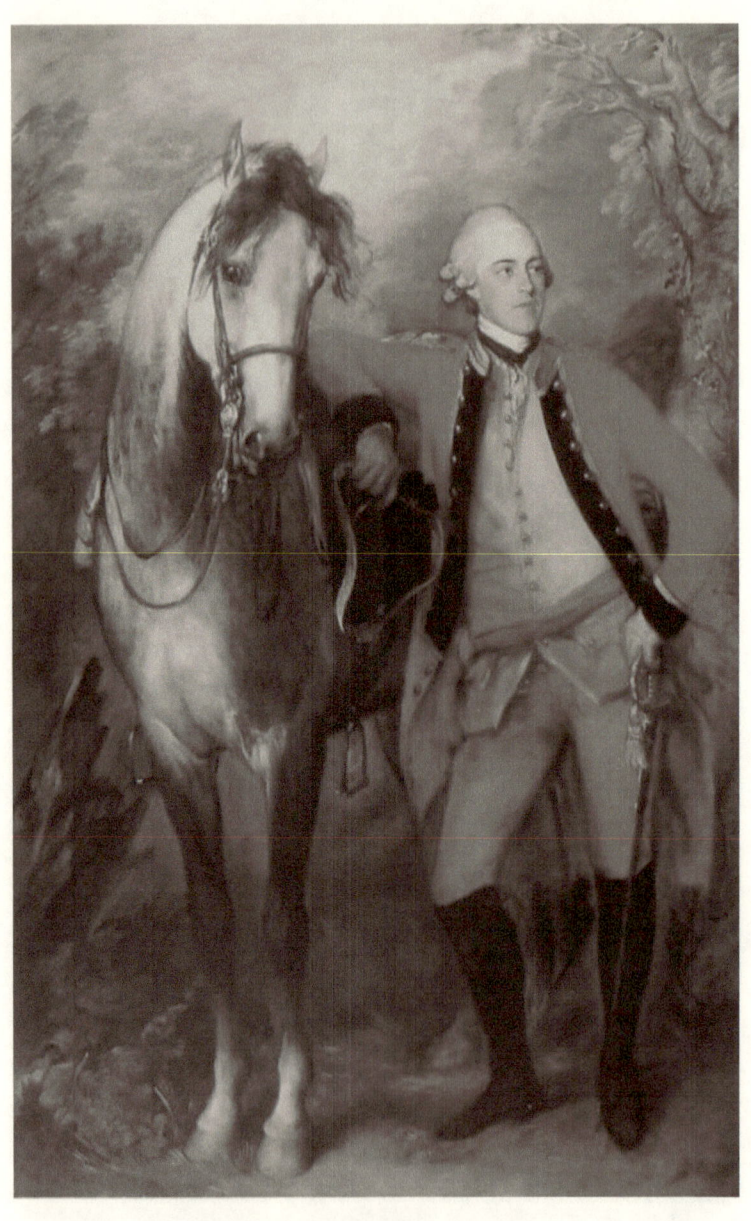

Edward, 2nd Viscount Ligonier, 1770, oil on canvas

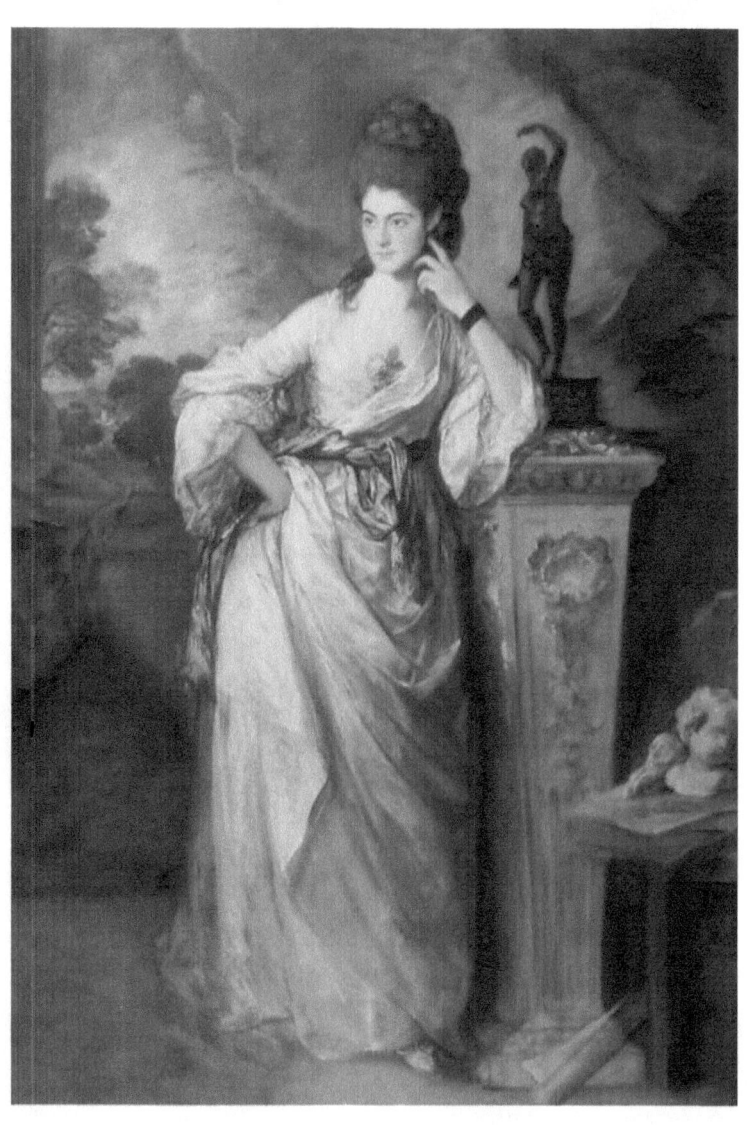

Lady Ligonier, 1770, oil on canvas

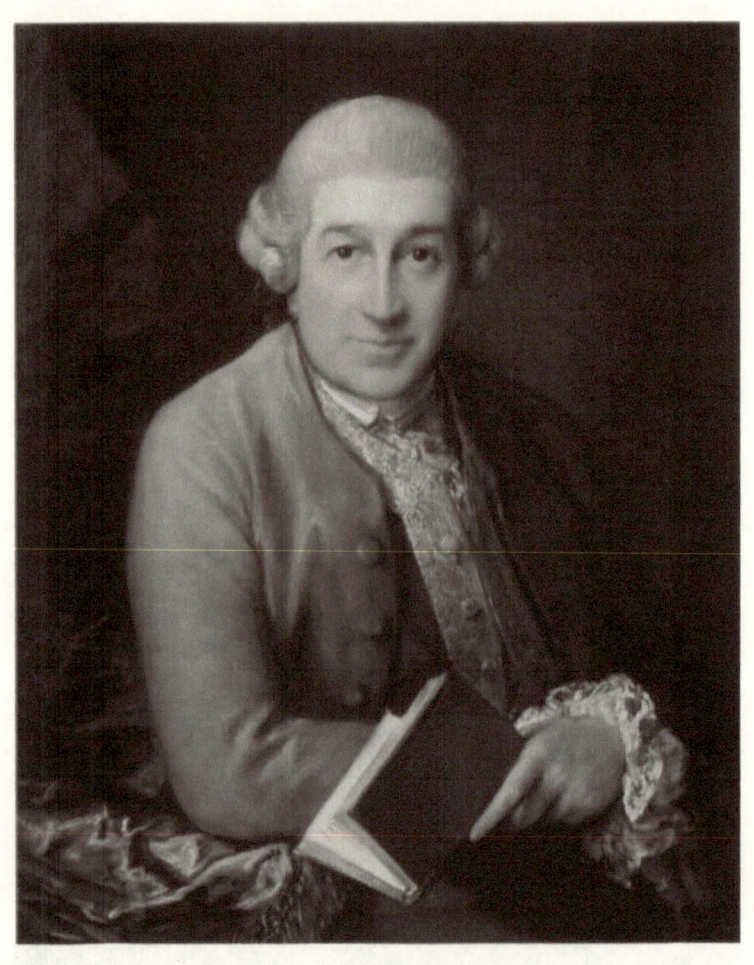

Portrait of David Garrick, 1770, oil on canvas

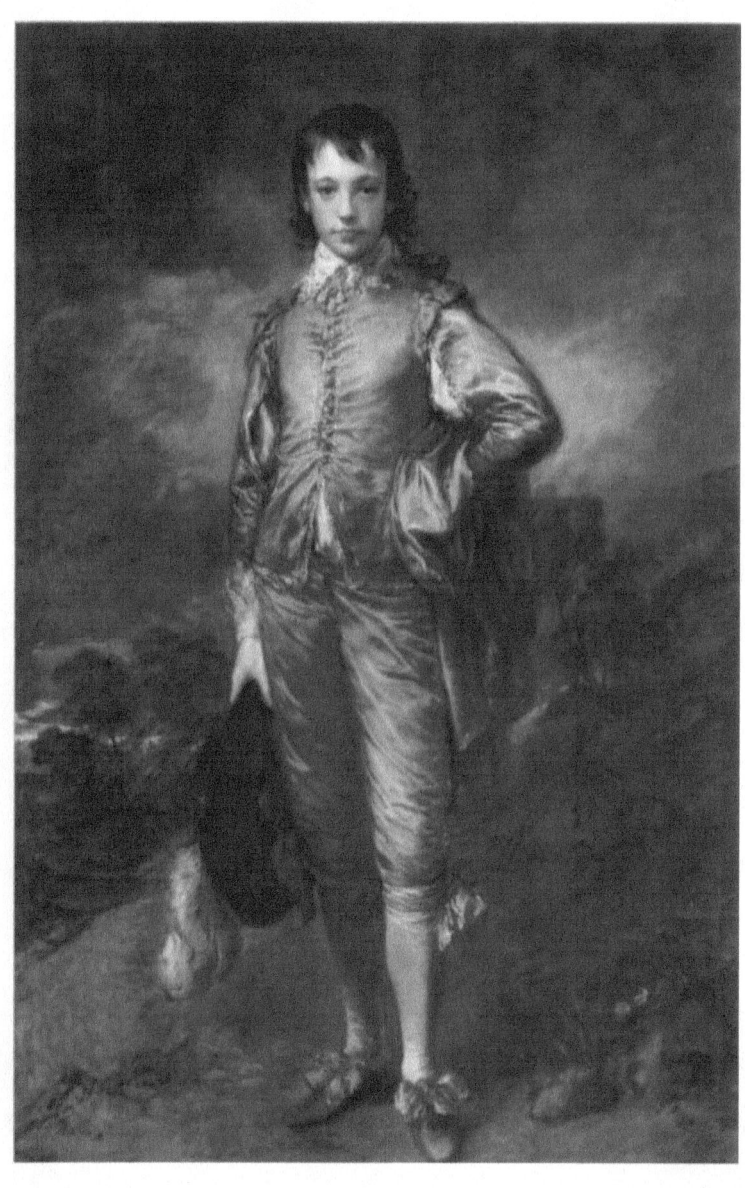

The Blue Boy (Portrait of the Jonathan Buttall), 1770, oil on canvas

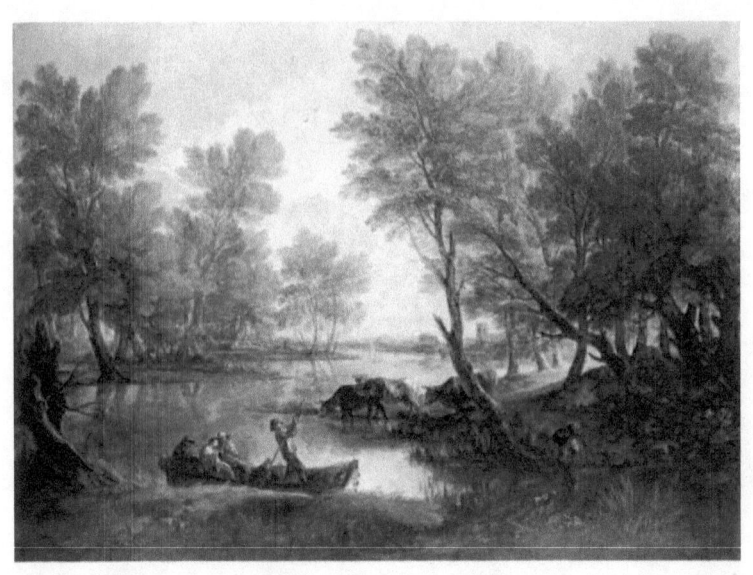

River landscape, 1770, oil on canvas

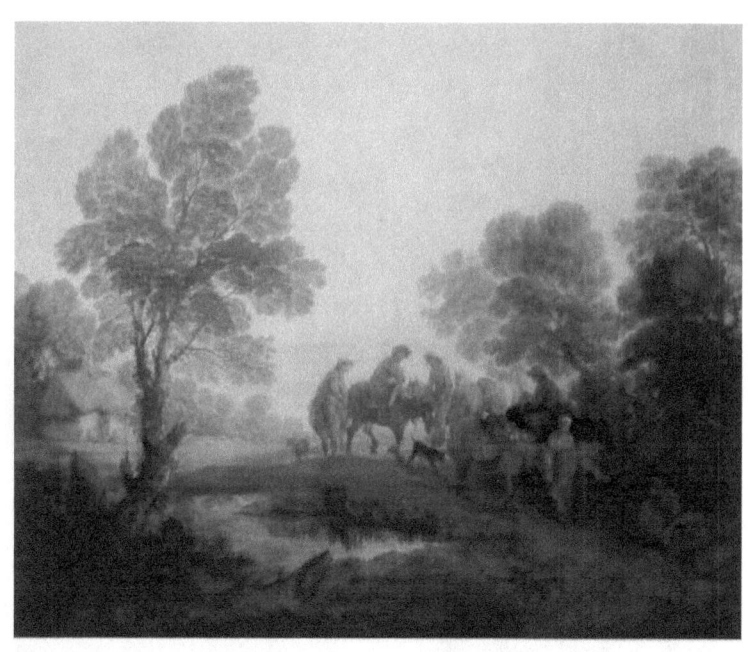

Evening Landscape Peasants and Mounted Figures,
1771, oil on canvas

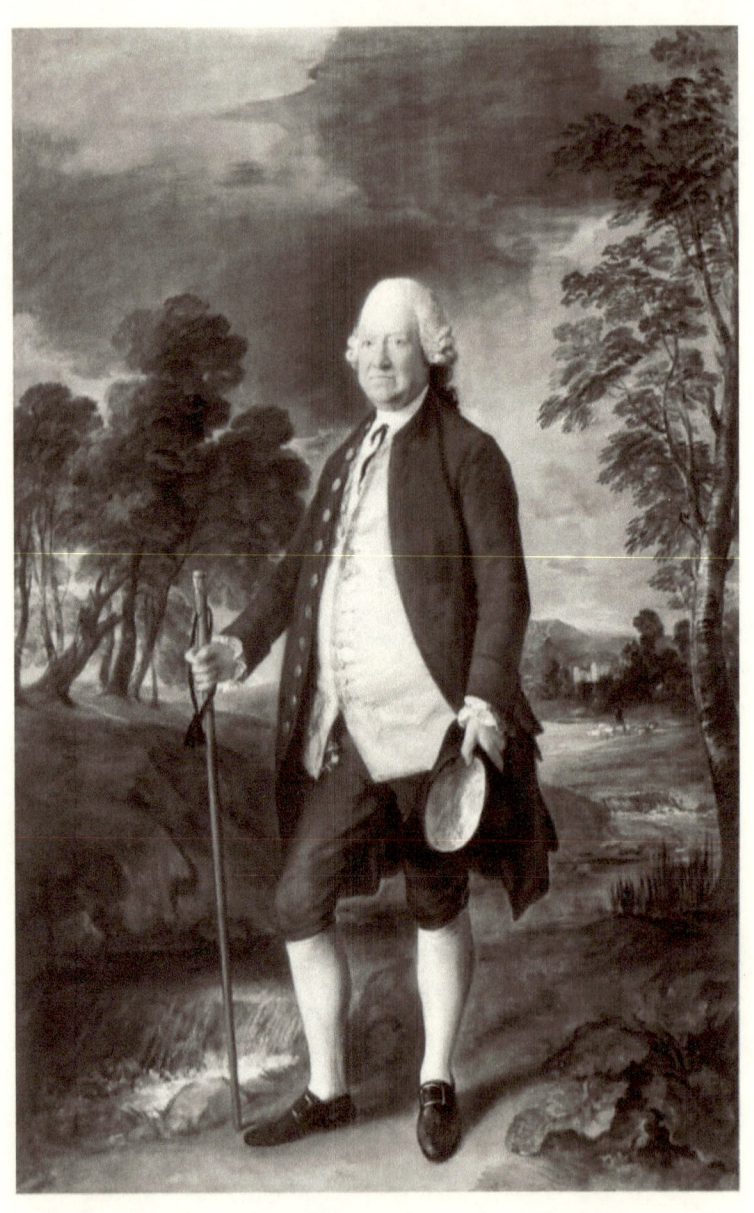

Benjamin Truman, 1774, oil on canvas

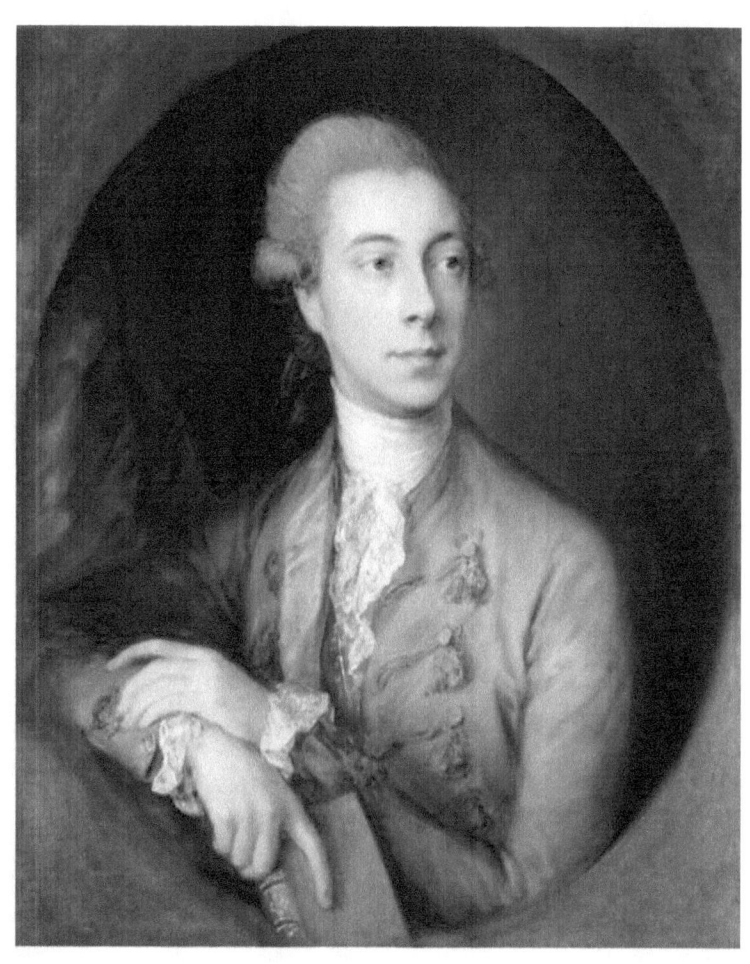

Richard Paul Jordell, c.1774, oil

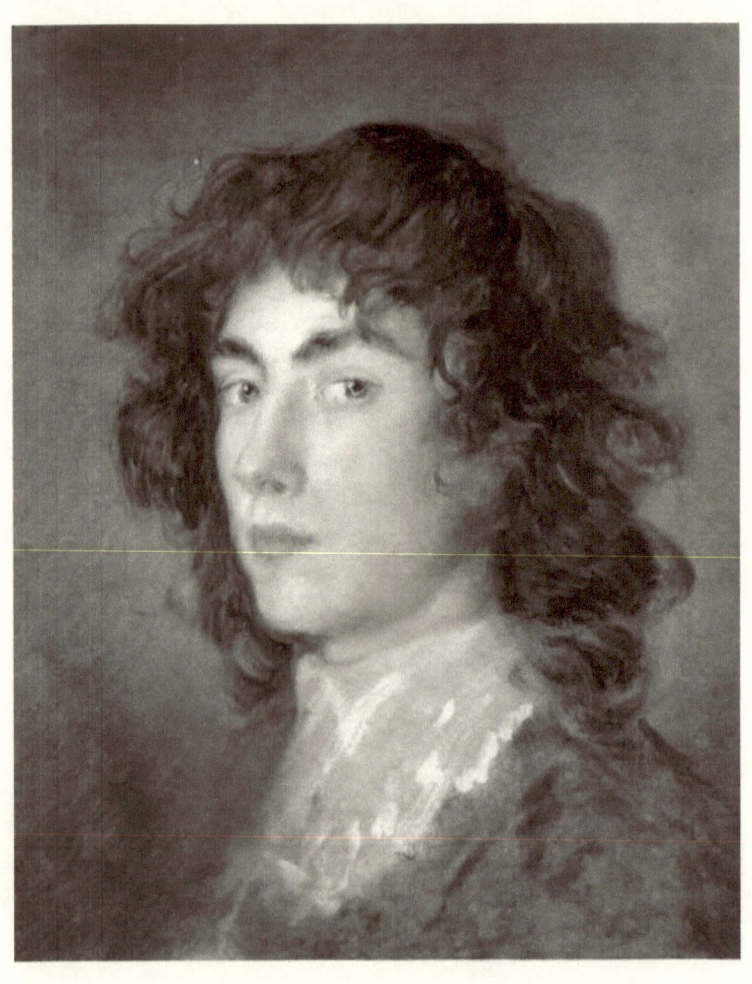

Dupont, 1775, oil on canvas

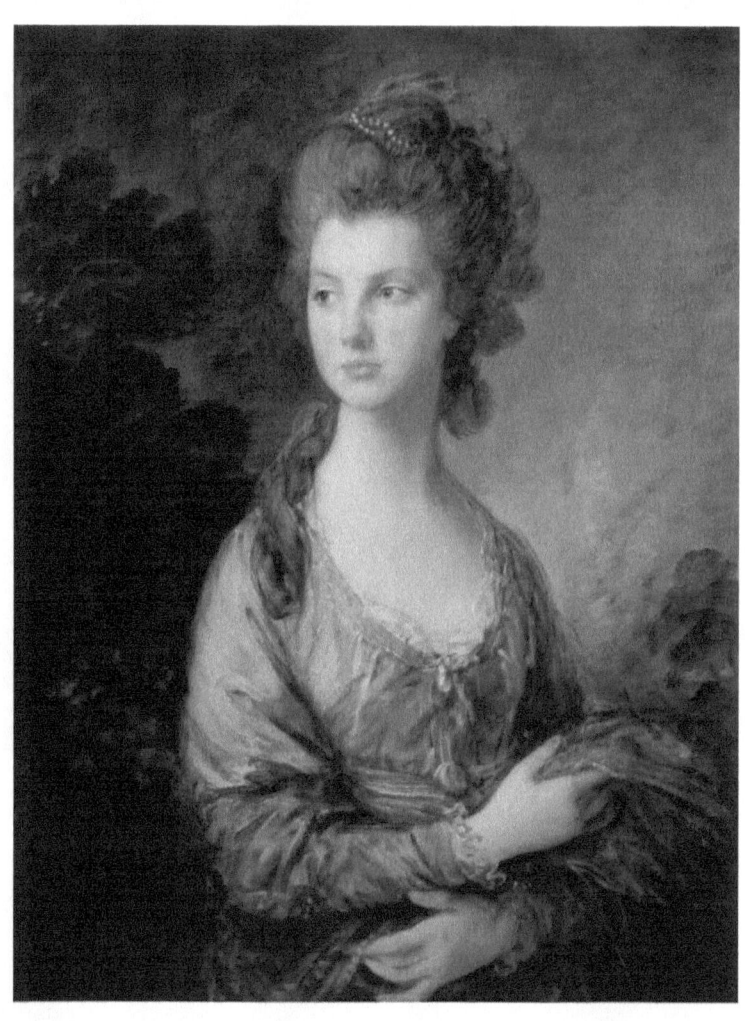

Mrs. Graham, 1775, oil on canvas

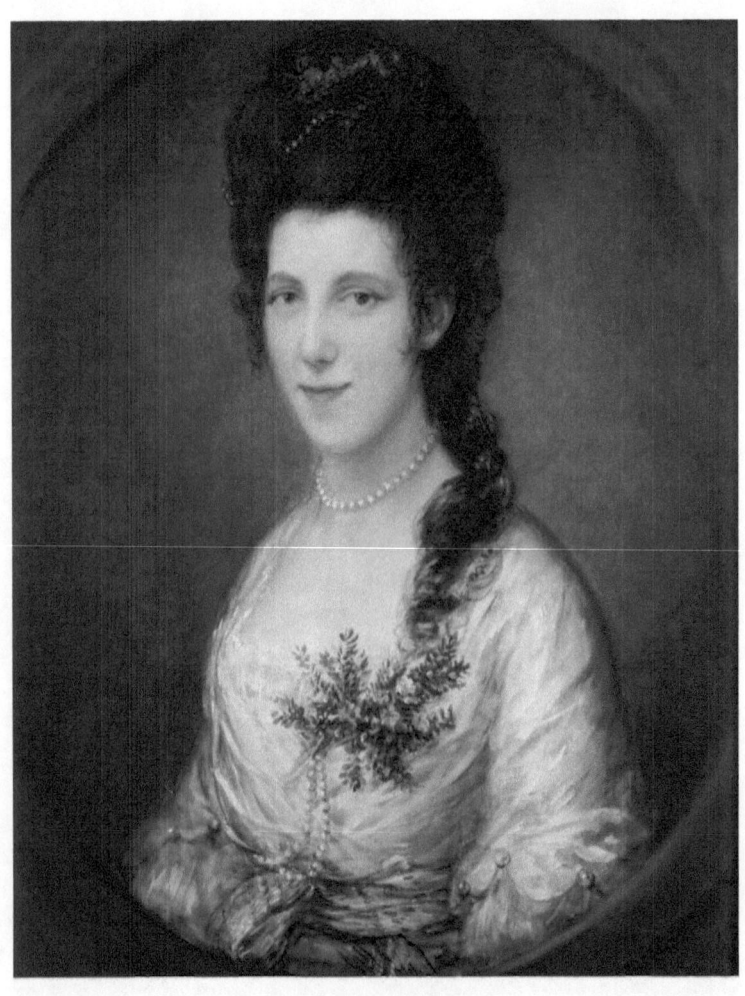

Portrait of a Lady (possibly Lady Eden), 1775, oil on canvas

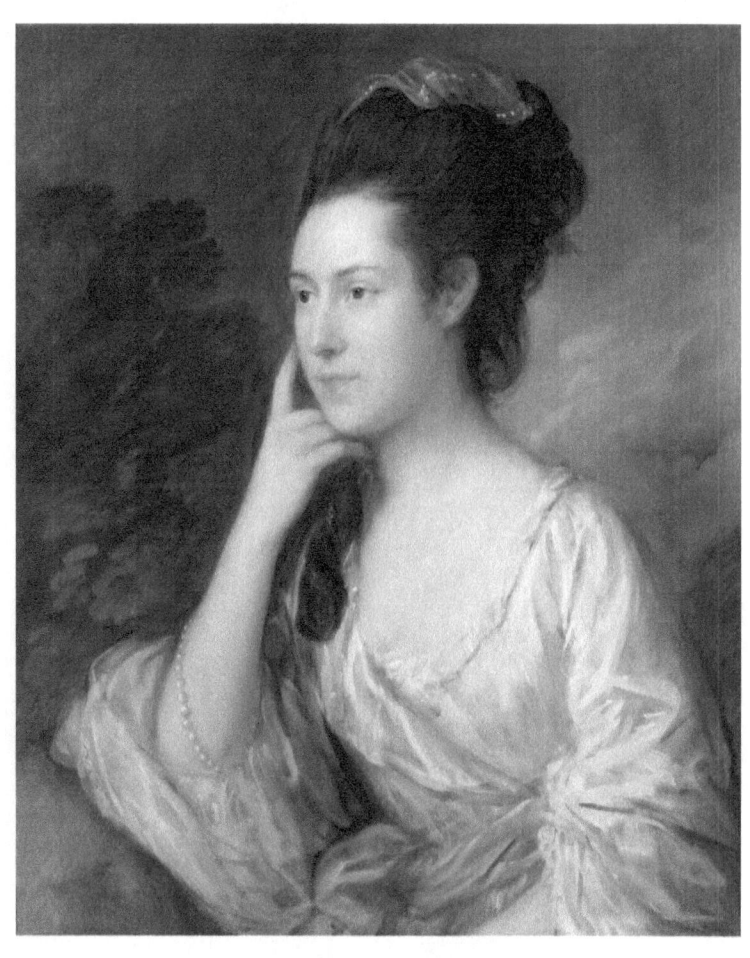

Portrait of Lady Chad, 1775, oil on canvas

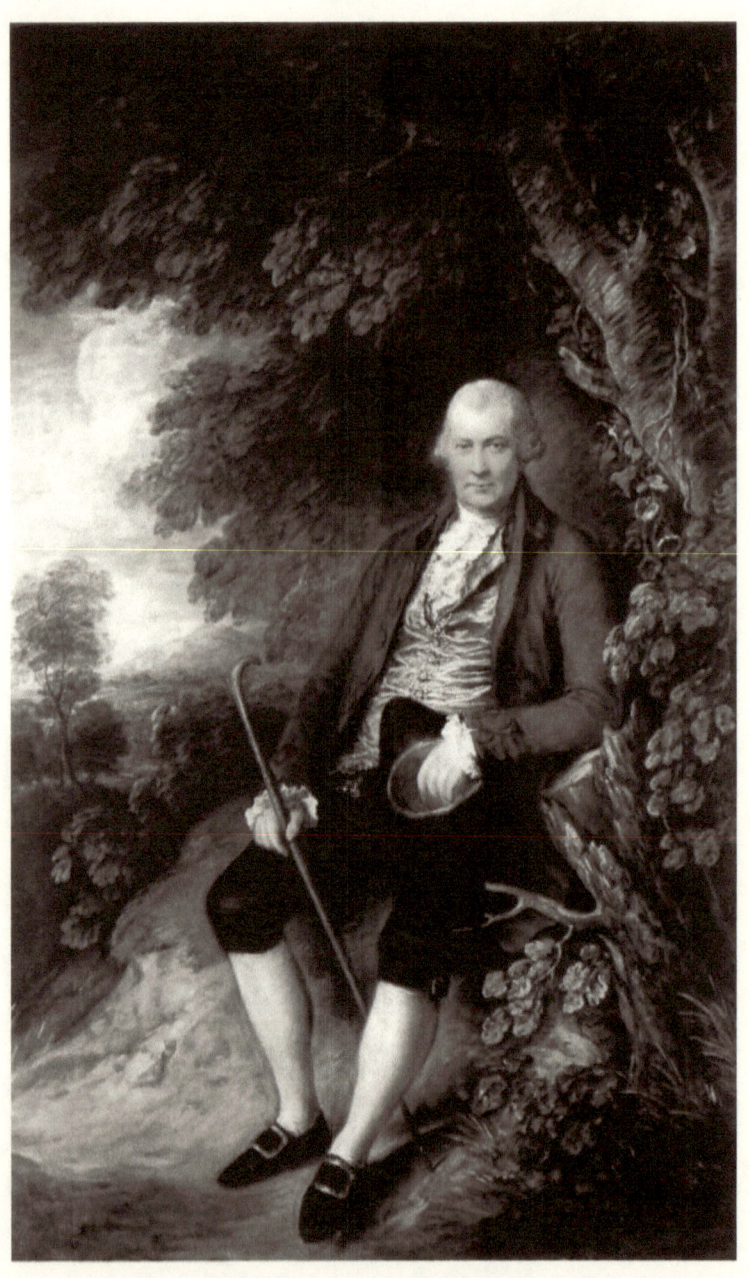

Squire John Wilkinson, 1776, oil on canvas

In this austere portrait of Squire John Wilkinson, late Gainsborough is seen at his best. Doubtless due to the sitter's demand, this likeness is relatively restrained, even the setting is less glamorised than usual for the painter's later phase (after 1774). Wilkinson, a manufacturer of cannon and founder of the British iron industry, was known as the 'Great Staffordshire Ironmaster'; he was a self-proclaimed atheist and follower of Tom Paine.

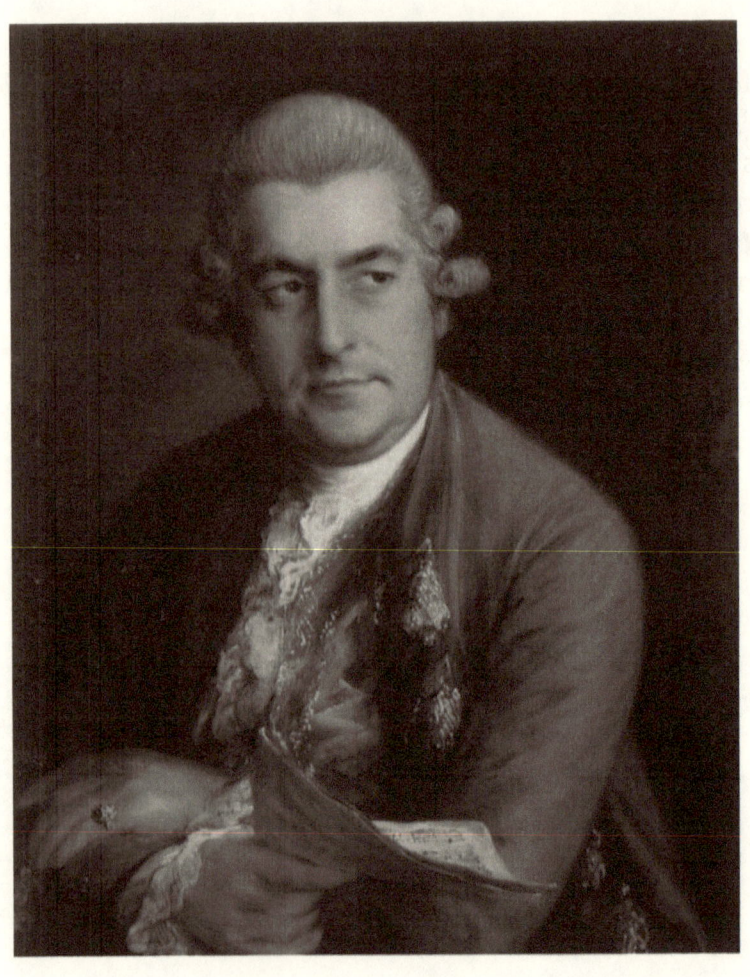

Johann Christian Bach, 1776, oil on canvas

The artist preferred the company of actors, artists, dramatists and musicians to that of politicians, writers or scholars, and was himself a talented amateur musician in addition to being a painter. Some of his finest portraits are of musicians and include the composer Karl Friedrich Abel (San Marino, Henry E. Huntington Library and Art Gallery) and Johann Christian Bach.

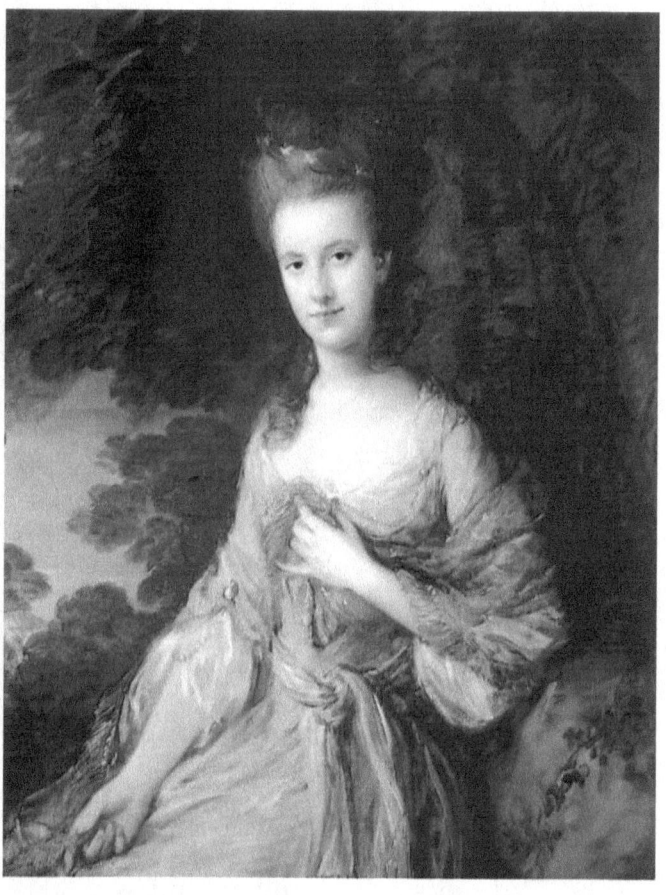

Portrait of Sarah Buxton, 1776-77, oil on canvas

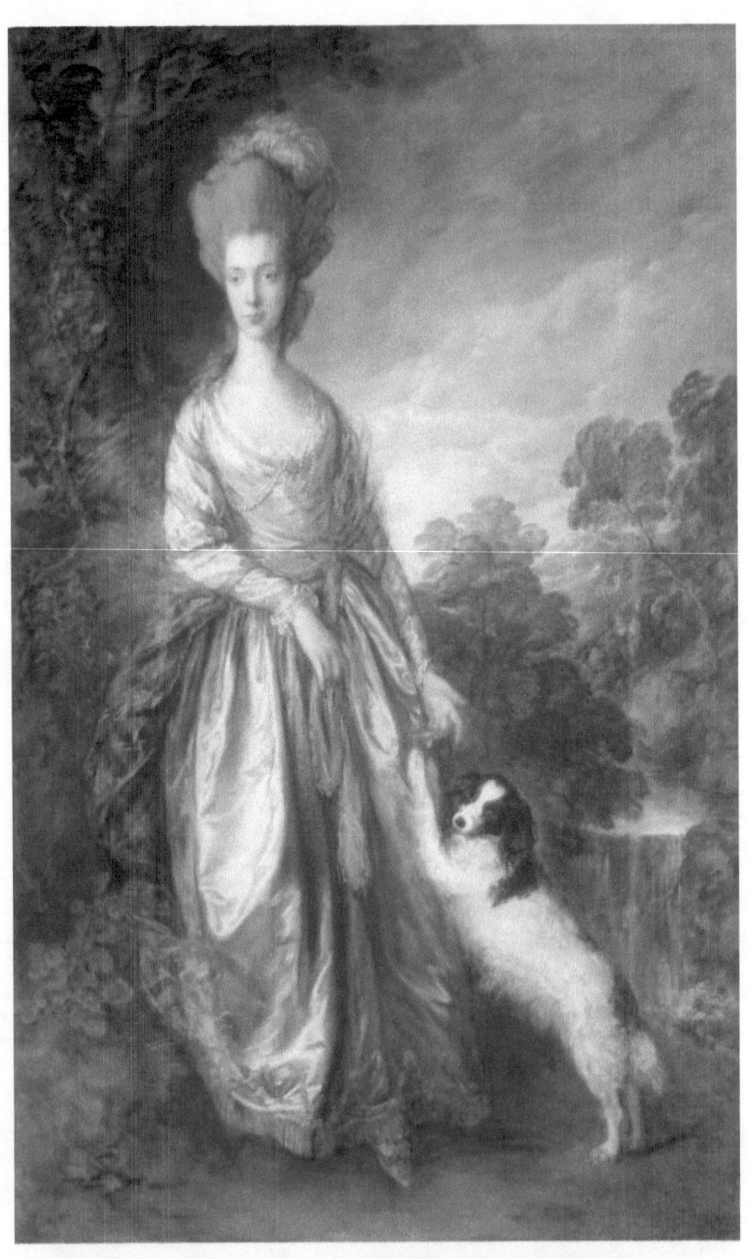

Lady Brisco, 1776, oil on canvas

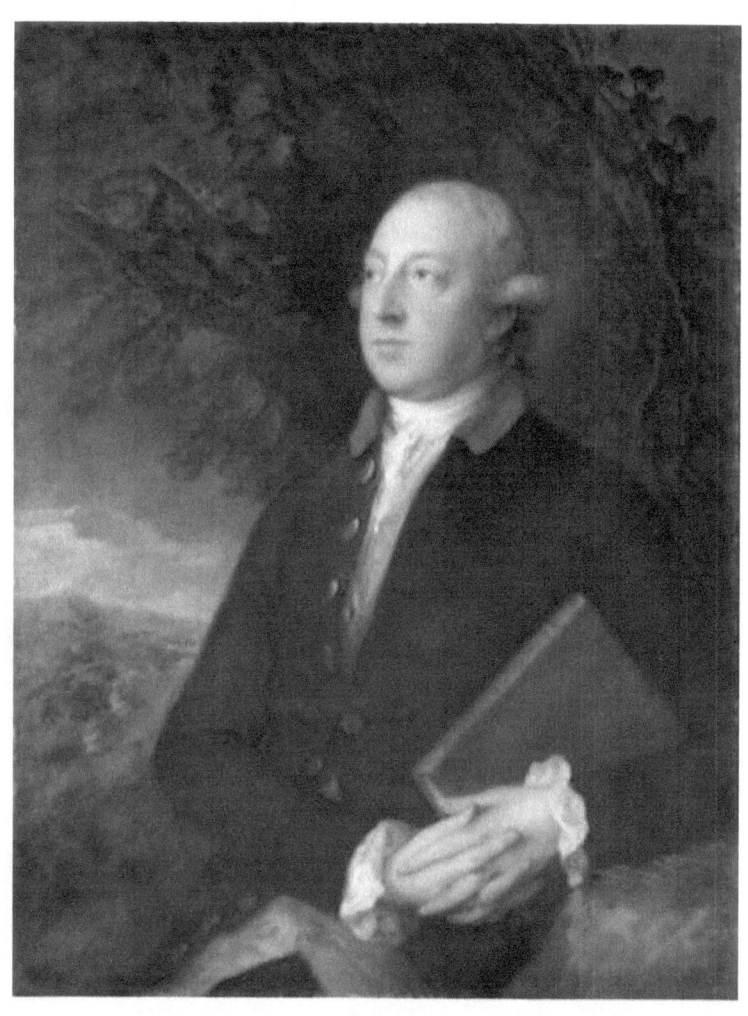

Thomas Pennant, 1776, oil

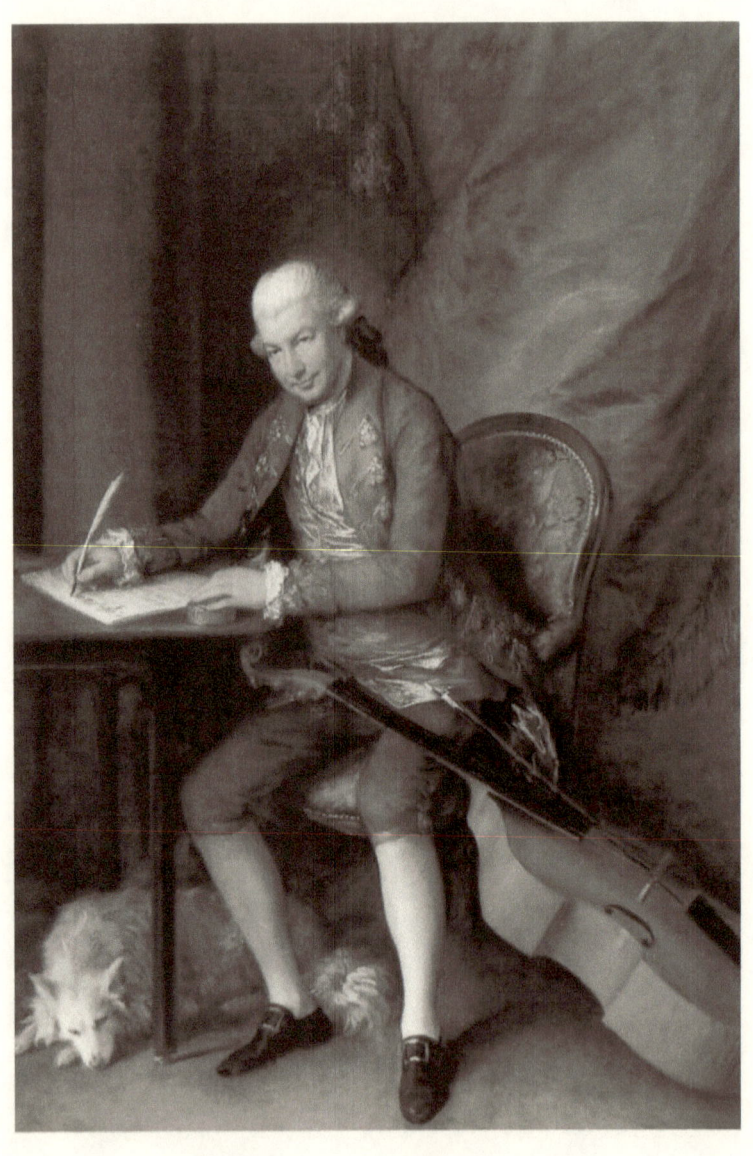

Carl Friedrich Abel, 1777, oil on canvas

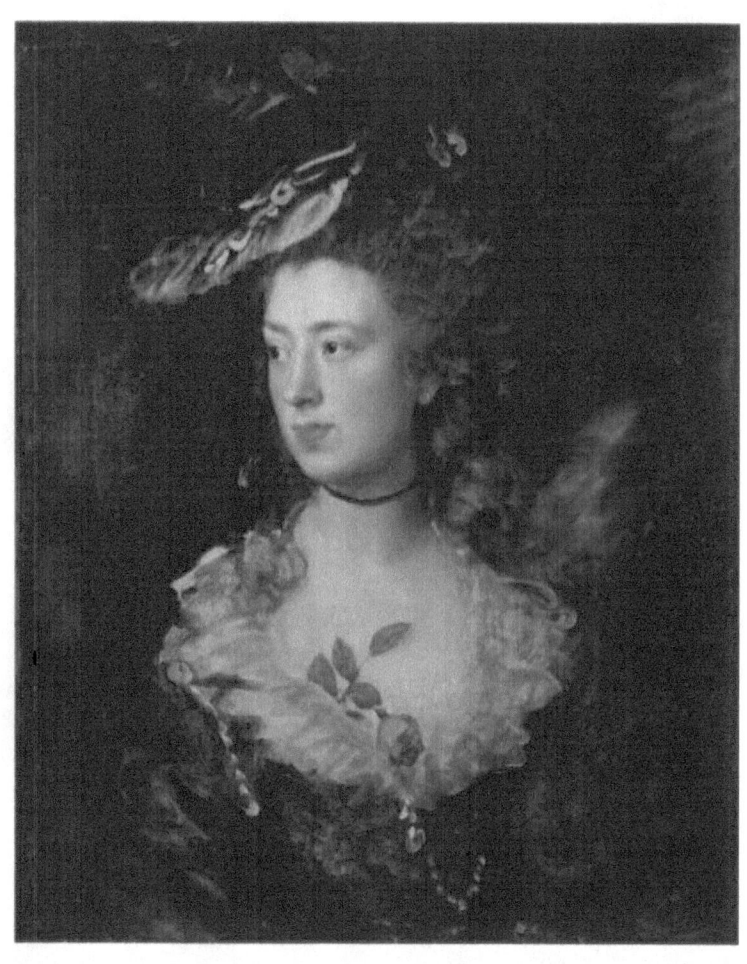

Portrait of the Mary Gainsborough, 1777, oil on canvas

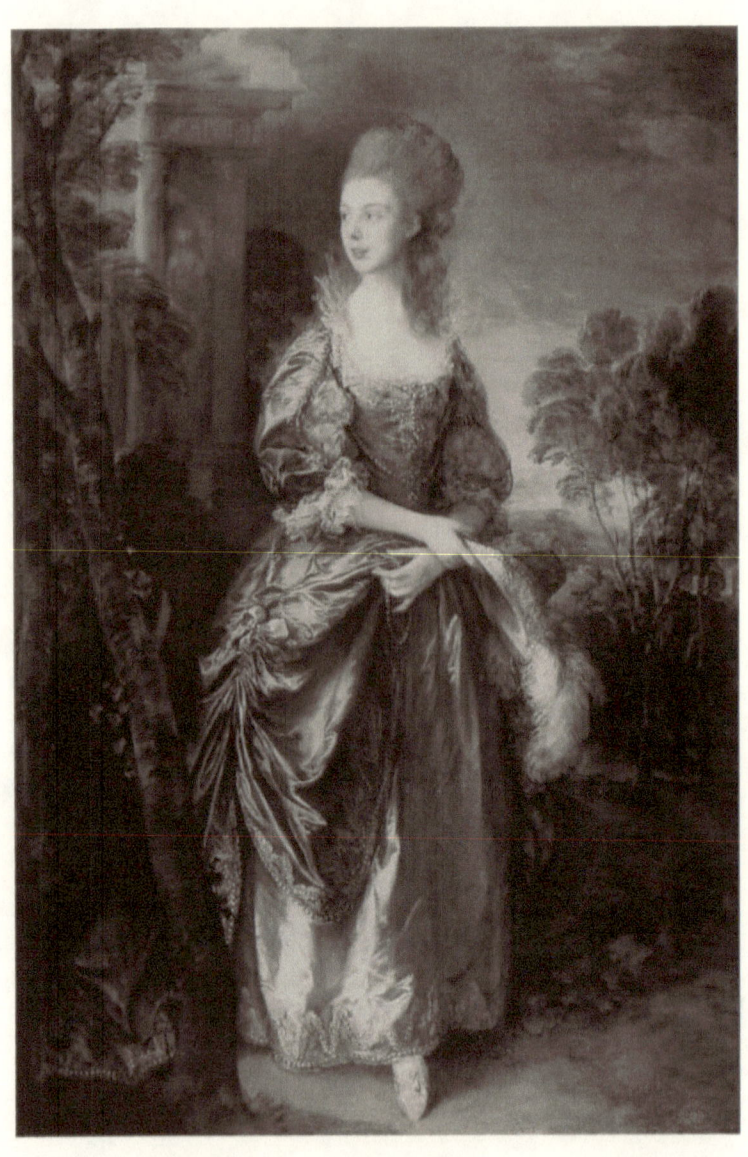

The Hon. Frances Duncombe, c.1777, oil

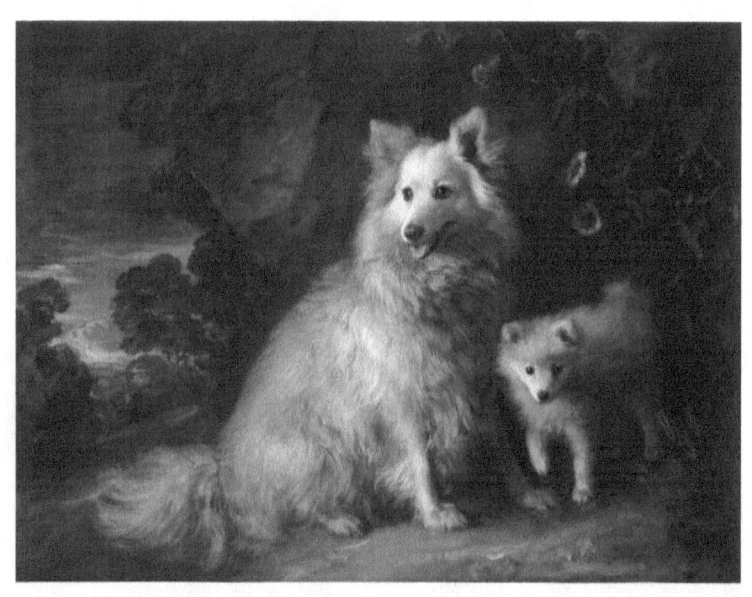

Pomeranian Bitch and Pup c.1777, oil

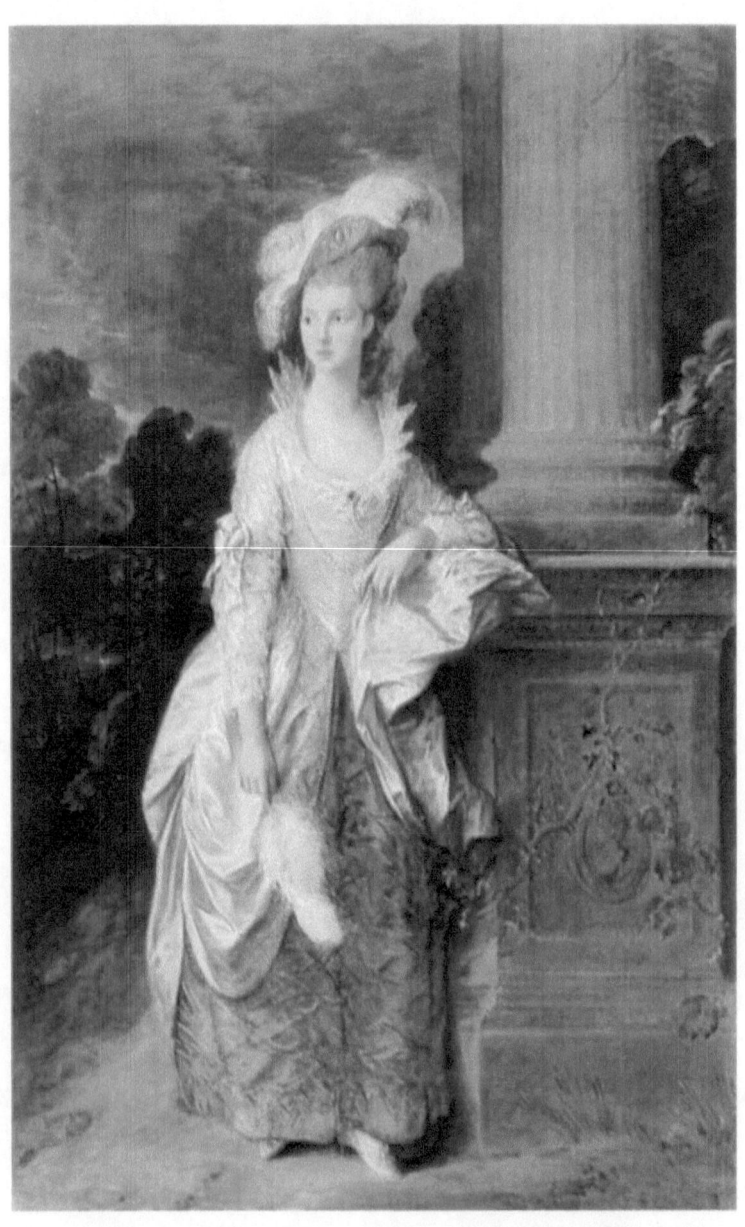

The Hon. Mrs. Graham, 1777, oil on canvas

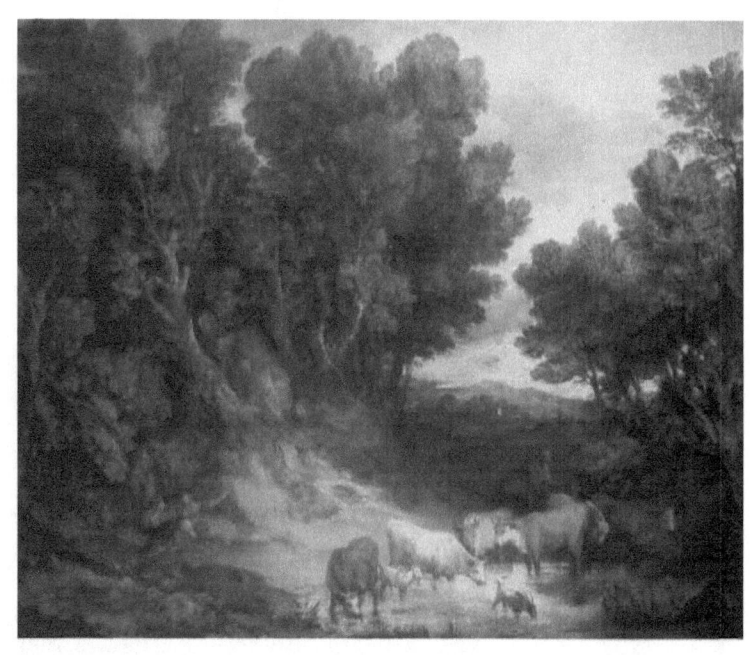

The Watering Place, 1777, oil on canvas

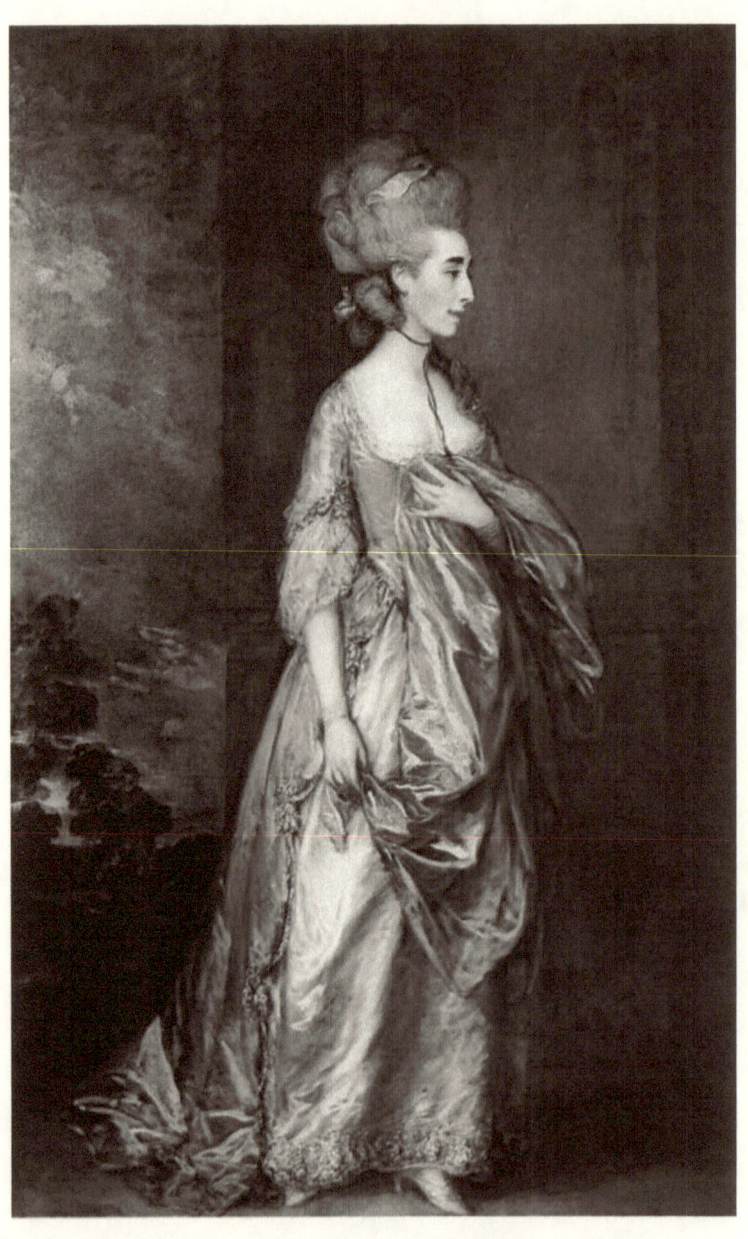

Mrs. Grace D. Elliott, 1778, oil on canvas

Thomas Gainsborough rivaled Sir Joshua Reynolds as the leading portrait painter of 18th-century England. He publicly stylised his opposition in art-theoretical questions, but remained in a good working relationship with Reynolds. Gainsborough had begun his career as a provincial painter in Suffolk by copying landscapes and portraying the landed gentry. From 1759 to 1774 he worked in the society resort of Bath, where a high-ranking, increasingly enthusiastic clientele gave him well-paid commissions. In 1768 Gainsborough was one of the founder-members of the Royal Academy of Arts, and the only portraitist who was not based in London. Still, that was where his exalted clientele lived, and so that was where he moved in 1774, profiting also from the patronage of the royal family.

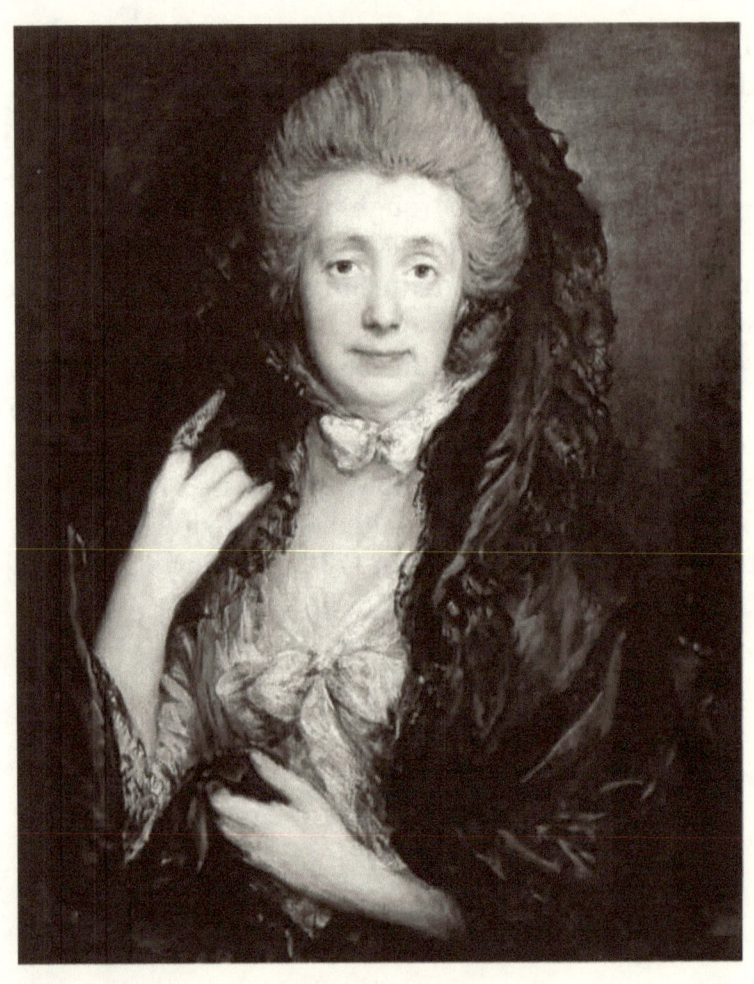

Nee Margaret Burr, 1778, oil on canvas

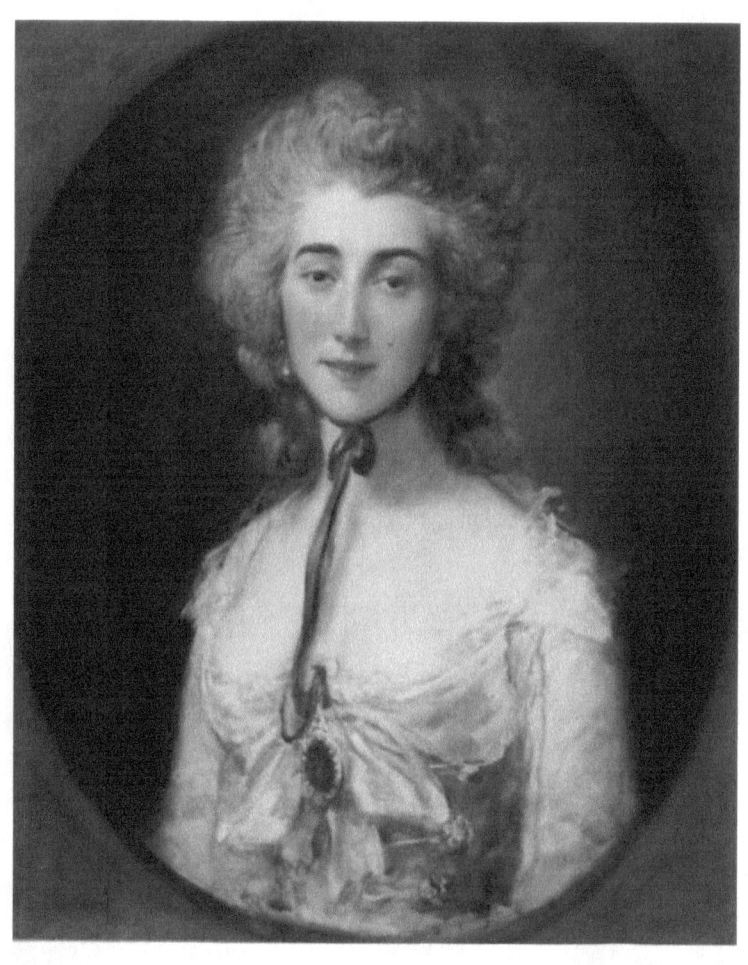

Portrait of Grace Dalrymple Elliott, 1778, oil on canvas

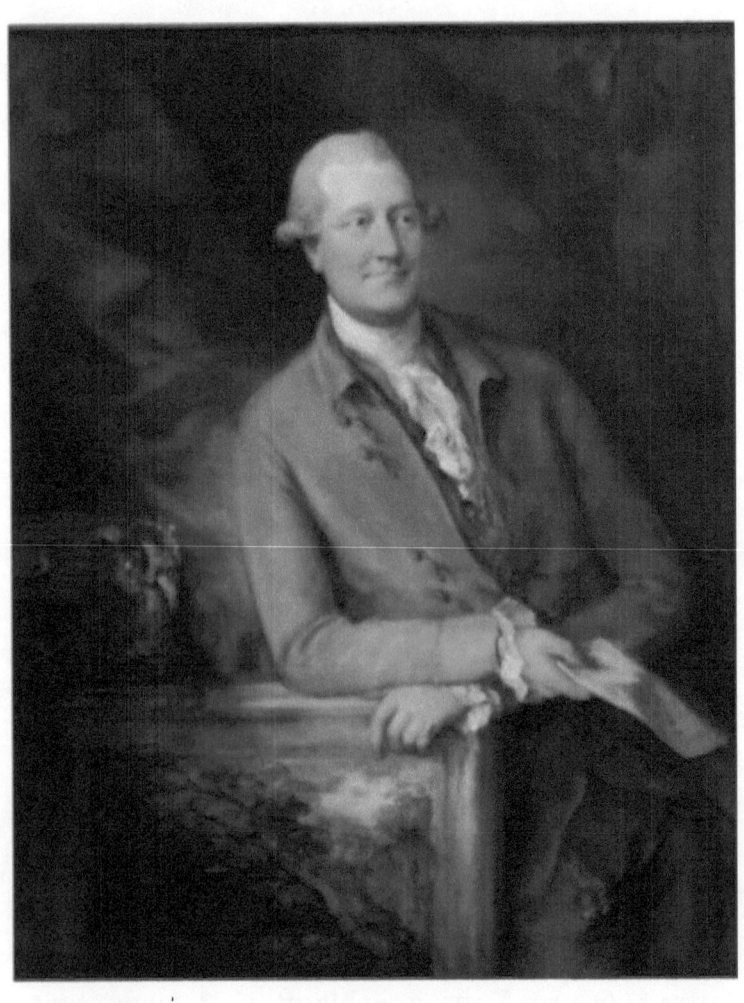

Portrait of James Christie, 1778, oil on canvas

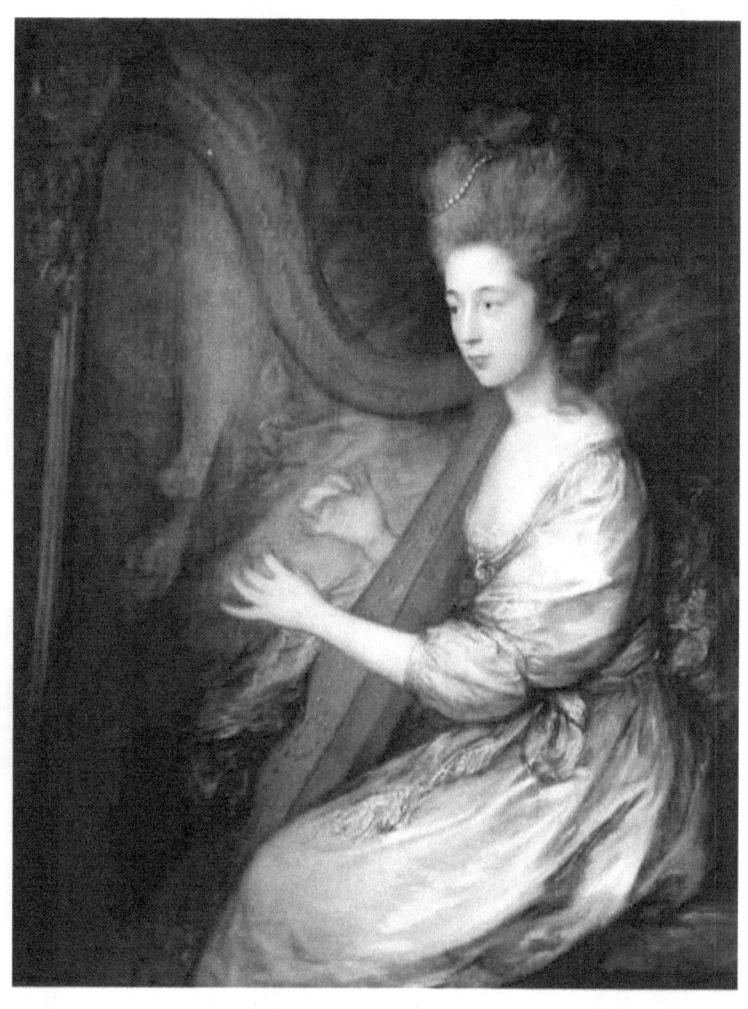

Portrait of Louisa, Lady Clarges, 1778, oil on canvas

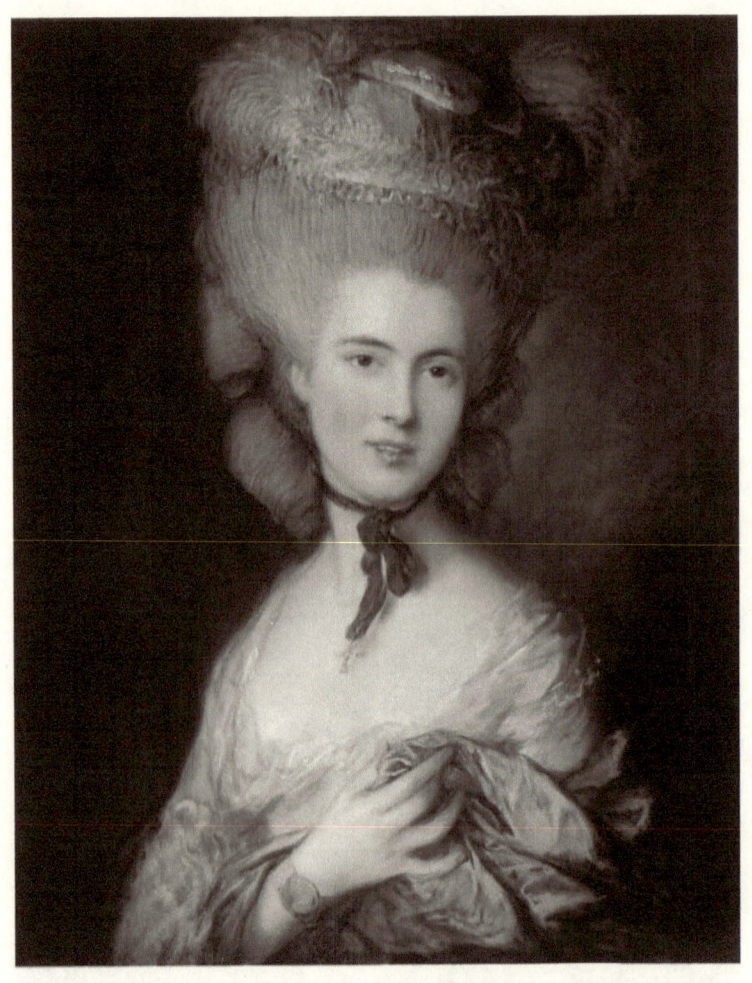

Portrait of a Lady in Blue, 1779-81, oil on canvas,

The vocation of Gainsborough, who spent most of his life outside the British capital, was landscape painting. In the studio he compiled real-life impressions, garnered during frequent strolls, into decorative compositions that recall the painted fantasies of French Rococo artist Antoine Watteau. Gainsborogh became famous for his portraits, however, which were prized especially for the exquisite consonance of their colours. This painting, whose subject is unknown, displays the artist's characteristic harmonious blend of hues, here white and blue.

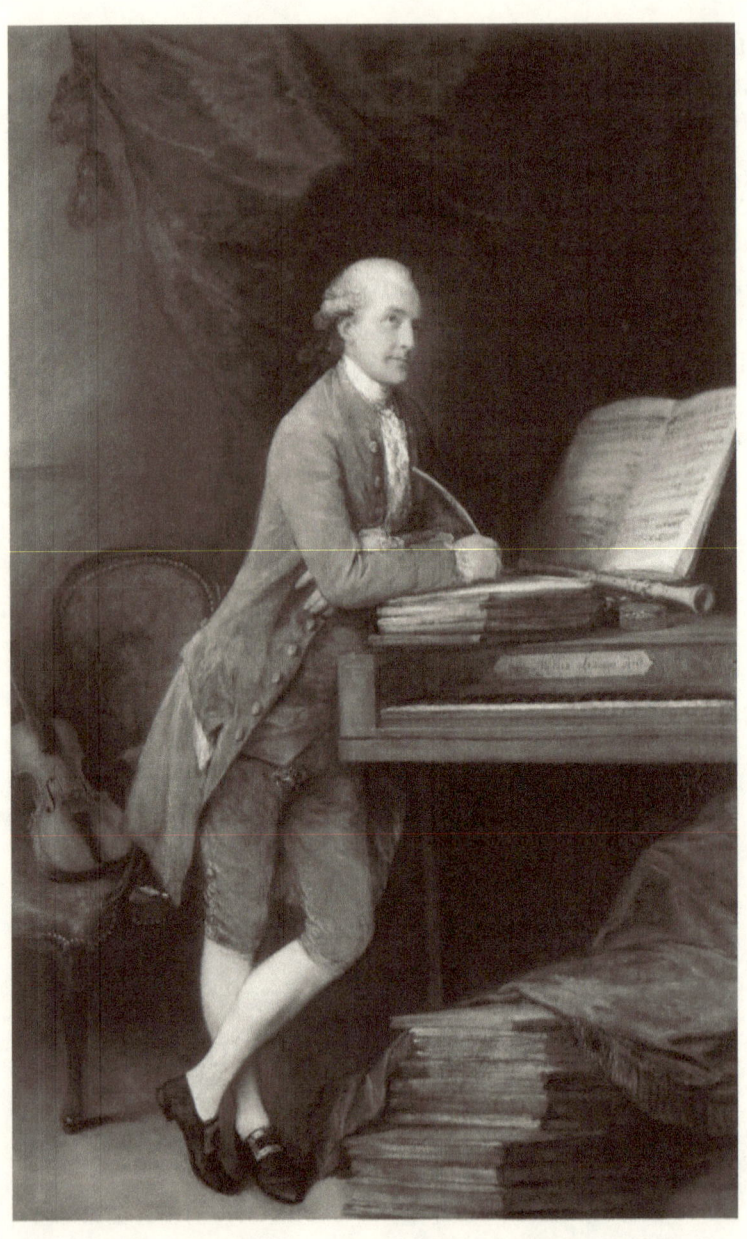

Johann Christian Fischer, 1780, oil on canvas

Johann Christian Fischer (1733-1800) was an outstanding musician. He was born in Germany at Freiburg-im-Breisgau and played for a time in the court band at Dresden before entering the service of Frederick the Great. On coming to London, where he is first recorded on 2 June 1768, he became a member of Queen Charlotte's Band and played regularly at court. His performance of Handel's fourth oboe concerto during the Handel Commemoration at Westminster Abbey in 1784 gave particular pleasure to George III. Regardless of such successes, he failed in 1786 to secure the post of Master of the King's Band. He collapsed in 1800 while playing in a concert at court and died shortly afterwards.

Fischer was a composer and virtuoso oboist. His two-keyed oboe is visible on the harpsichord-cum-piano against which the musician leans. Fanny Burney praised the 'sweet-flowing, melting celestial notes of Fischer's hautboy,' but the Italian violinist Felice de' Giardini (1716-93) referred to Fischer's 'impudence of tone as no other instrument could contend with.' In the portrait on the chair behind Fischer is a violin, on which he was apparently also an accomplished performer although only in private. The harpsichord-cum-piano, made by Joseph Merlin who came to London from the Netherlands in 1760 and established a successful business in the production of pianofortes, presumably refers to his abilities as a composer, as no doubt do the piles of musical scores.

This portrait of Johann Christian Fischer stands as testimony to Gainsborough's own love of music. The artist preferred the company of actors, artists, dramatists and musicians to that of politicians, writers or scholars, and was himself a talented amateur musician in addition to being a painter. Gainsborough once wrote to William Jackson: 'I'm sick of Portraits and wish very much to take my Viol da Gamba and walk off to some sweet Village when I can paint Landskips and enjoy the fag End of Life in quietness and ease.' Yet some of his finest portraits are of musicians and include, in addition to that of Fischer, the composer Karl Friedrich Abel (San Marino, Henry E. Huntington Library and Art Gallery) and Johann Christian Bach. These two portraits date from the late 1770s, whereas that of Johann Christian Fischer was exhibited at the Royal Academy in 1780.

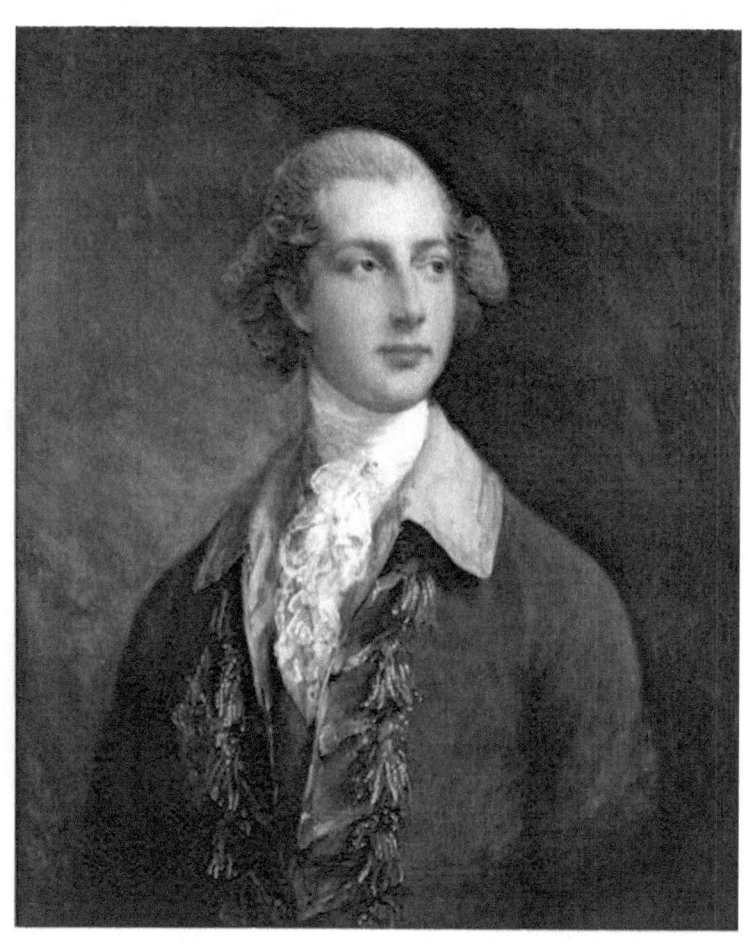

George IV as Prince of Wales, 1781, oil

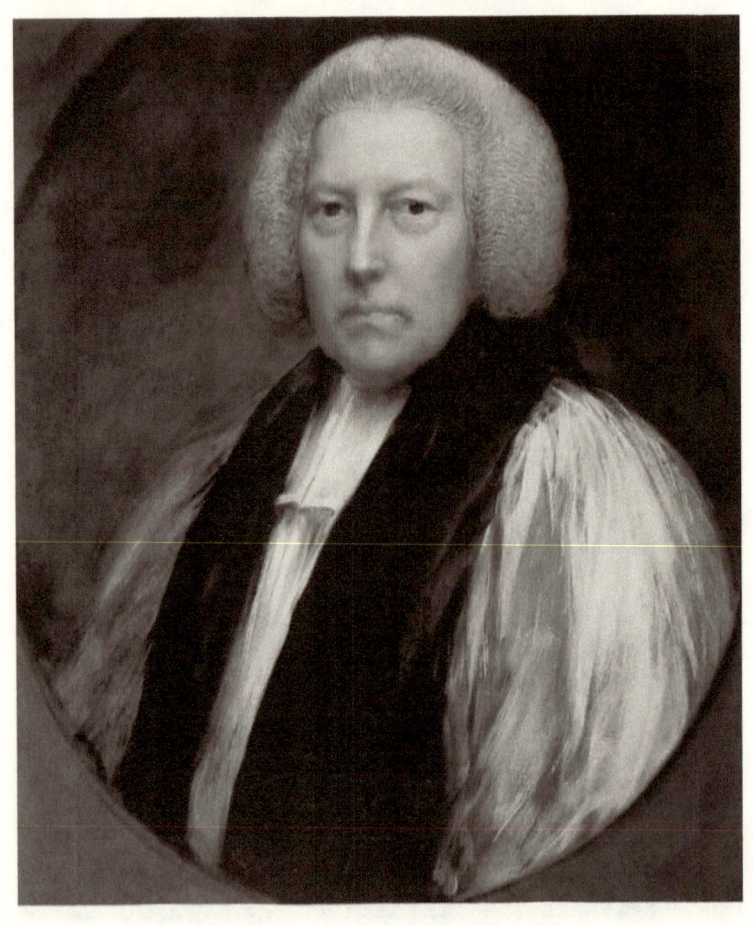

Richard Hurd, Bishop of Worcester, 1781, oil on canvas

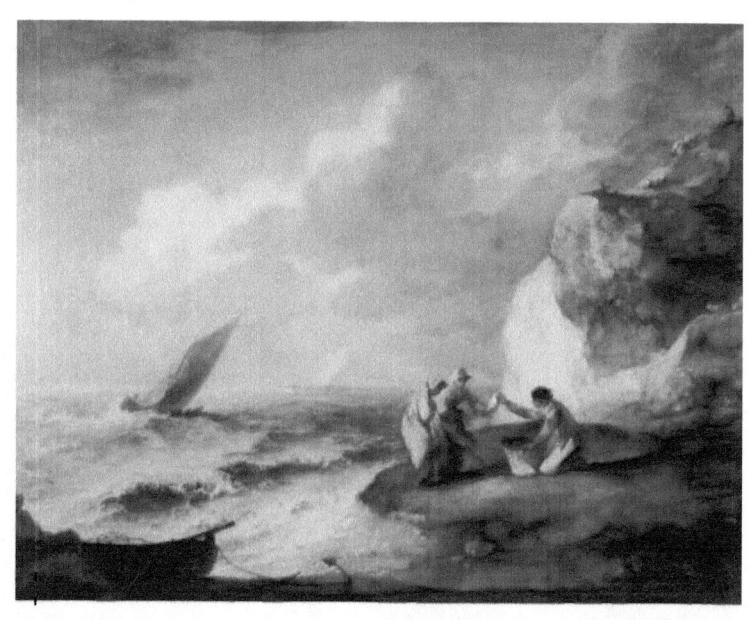

Rocky Coastal Scene, 1781, oil on canvas

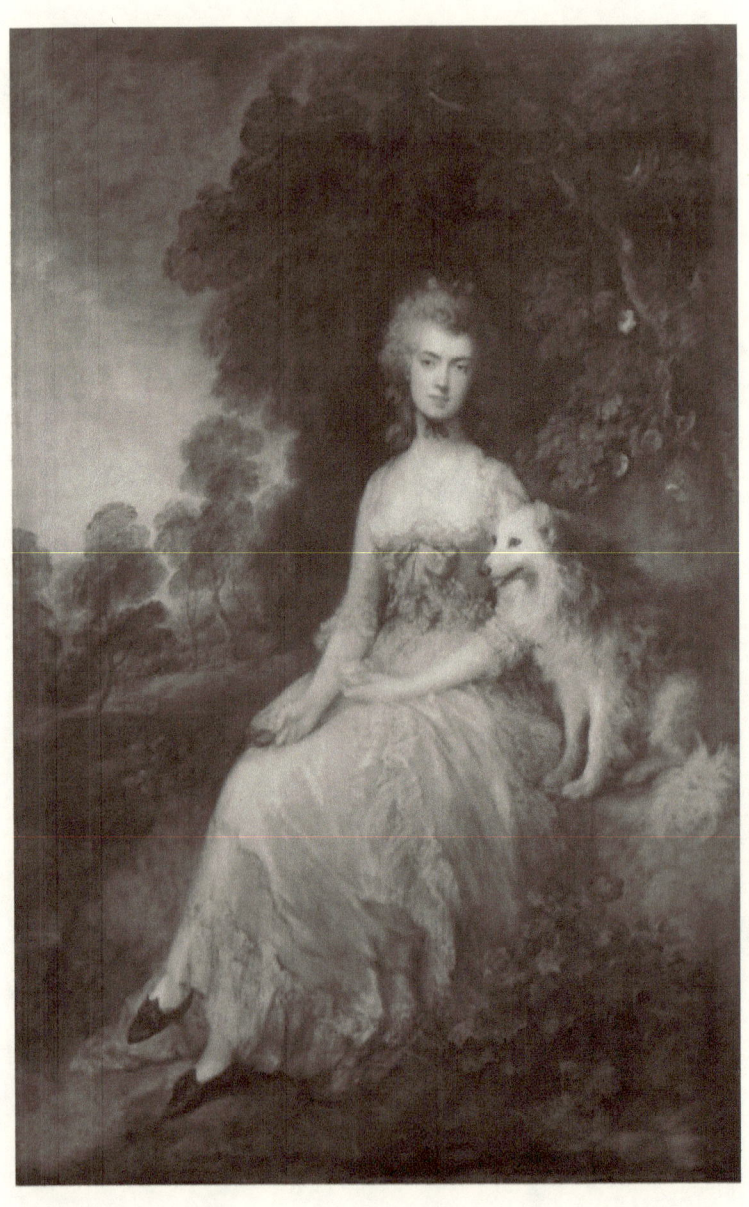

Mrs. Mary Robinson ("Perdita"), 1781, oil on canvas,

Mary Robinson, née Darby (1757-1800) was an English poet and novelist. She was also known for her role as Perdita (heroine of Shakespeare's The Winter's Tale) in 1779. It was during this performance that she attracted the notice of the young Prince of Wales, later King George IV of Great Britain and Ireland. Her affair with him ended in 1781, and "Perdita" Robinson was left to support herself through an annuity granted by the Crown (in return for some letters written by the Prince) in 1783 and through her writings. Today, she is remembered both as the first public mistress of George IV, and as a woman writer of the late 18th century.

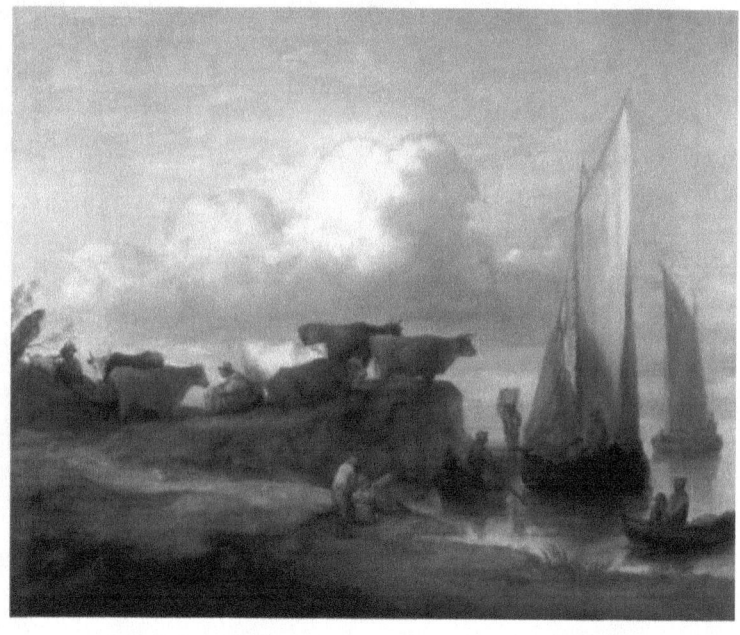

A Coastal Landscape, 1782, oil on canvas

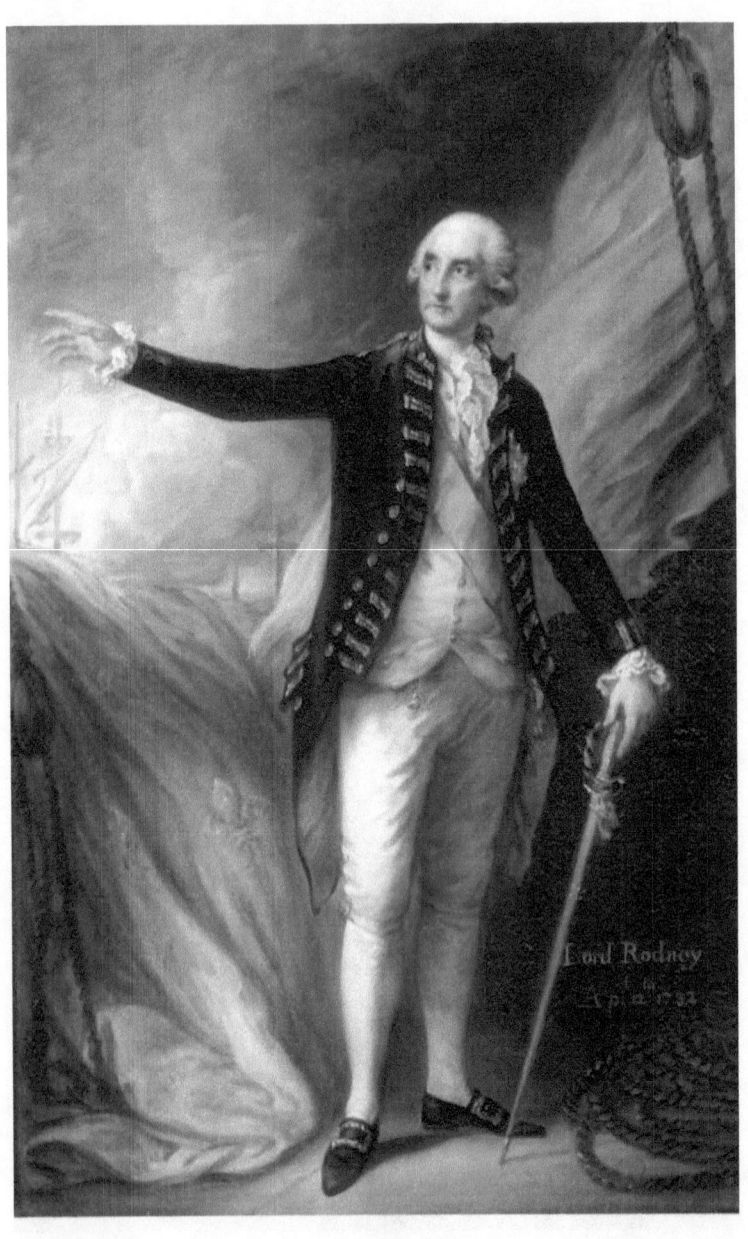

George Brydges Rodney, Admiral of the White, 1782,
oil on canvas

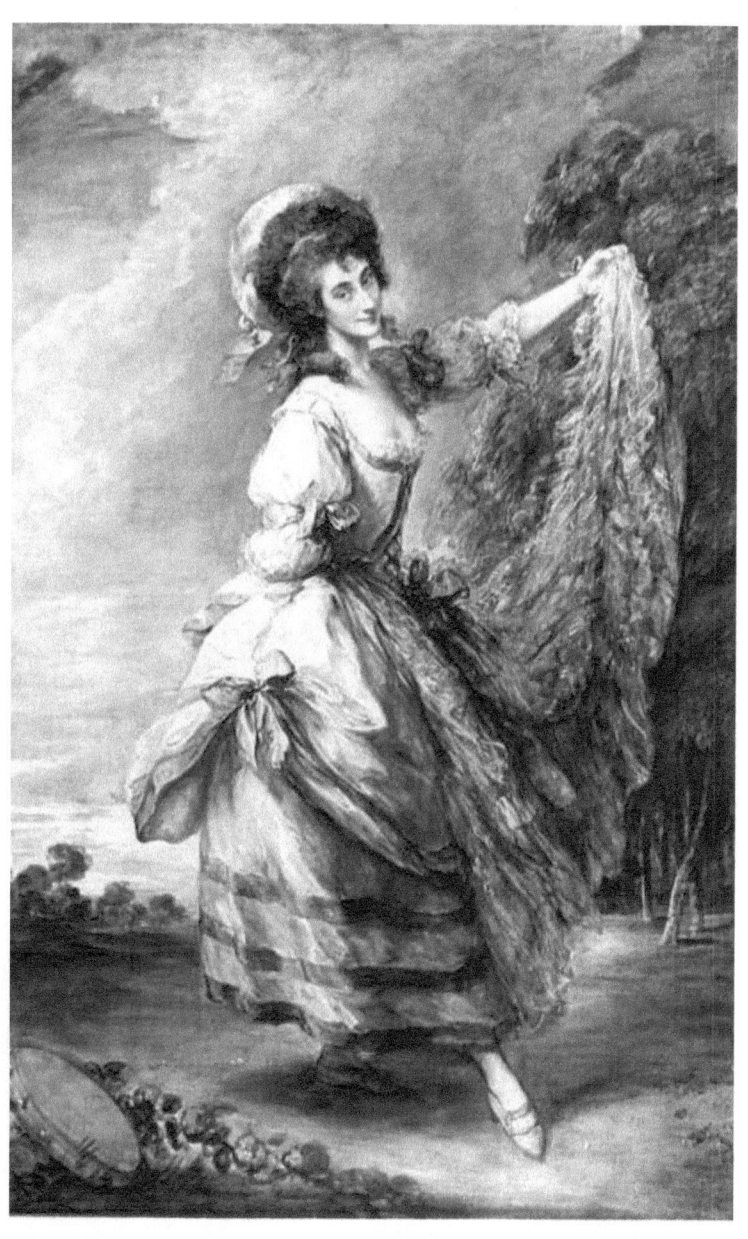

Giovanna Baccelli, 1782, oil on canvas

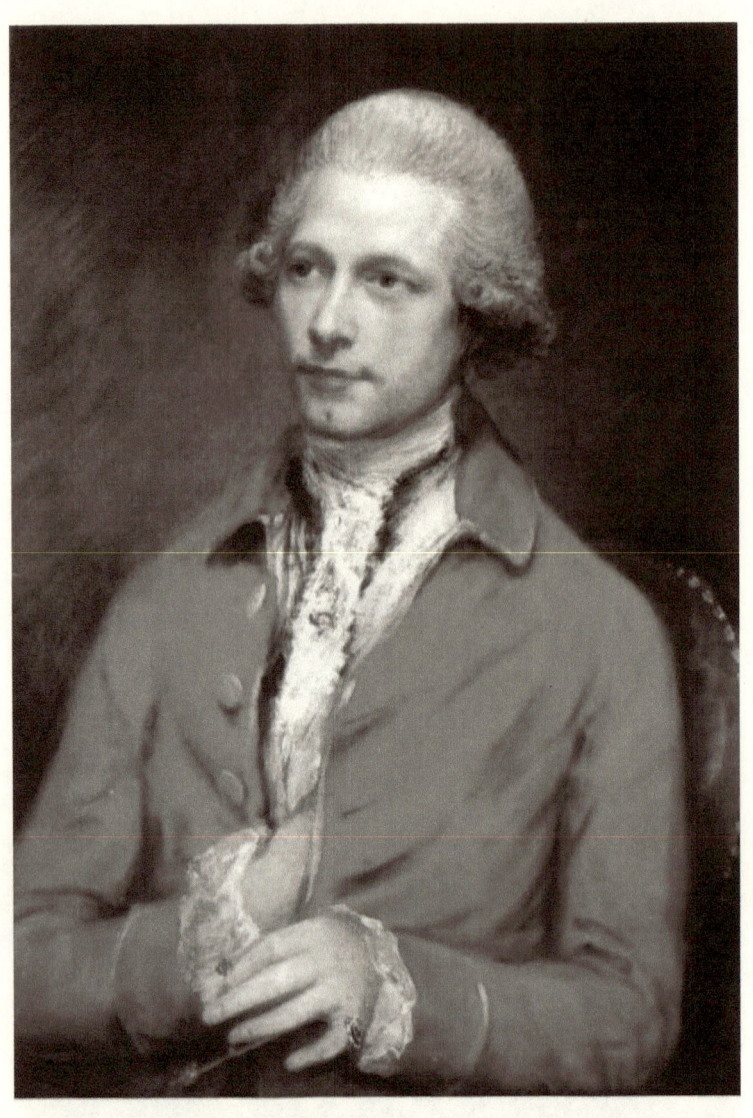

John Joseph Merlin, 1782, oil on canvas

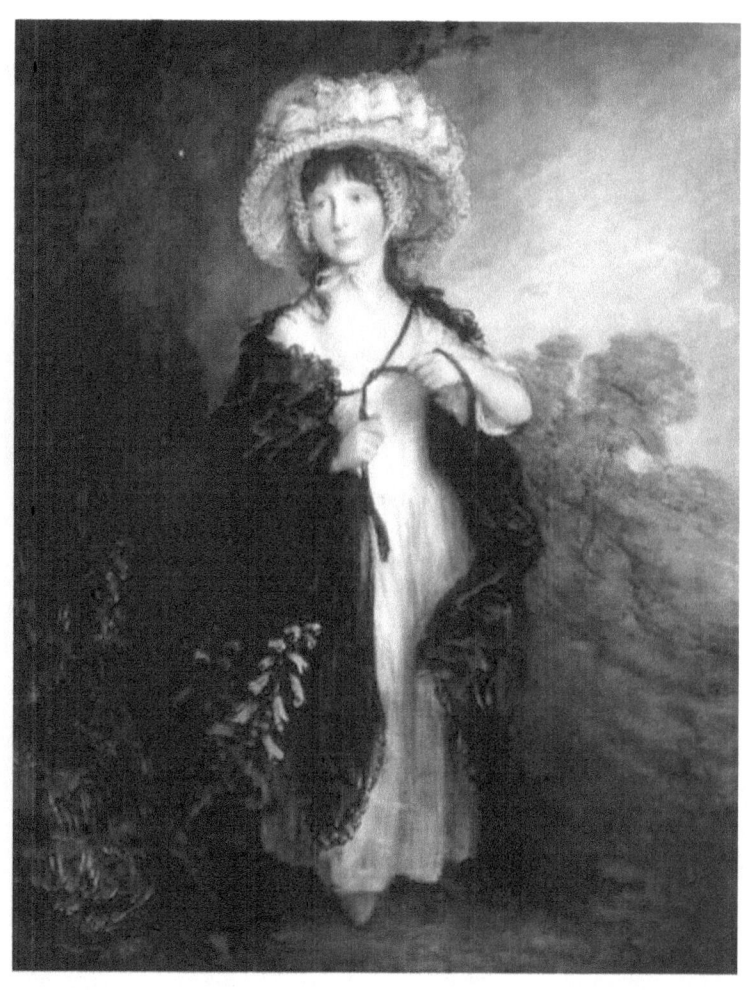

Miss Elizabeth Haverfield, 1782, oil on canvas

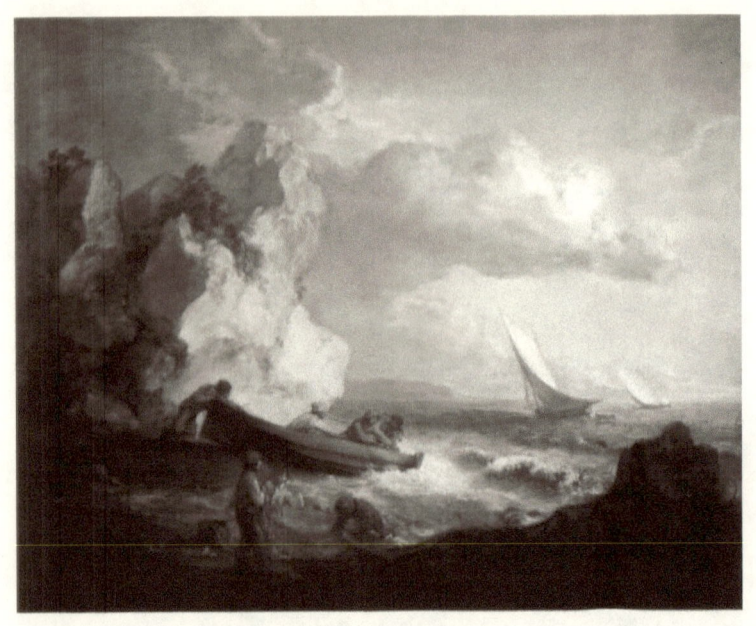

Seashore with Fishermen, 1782, oil on canvas

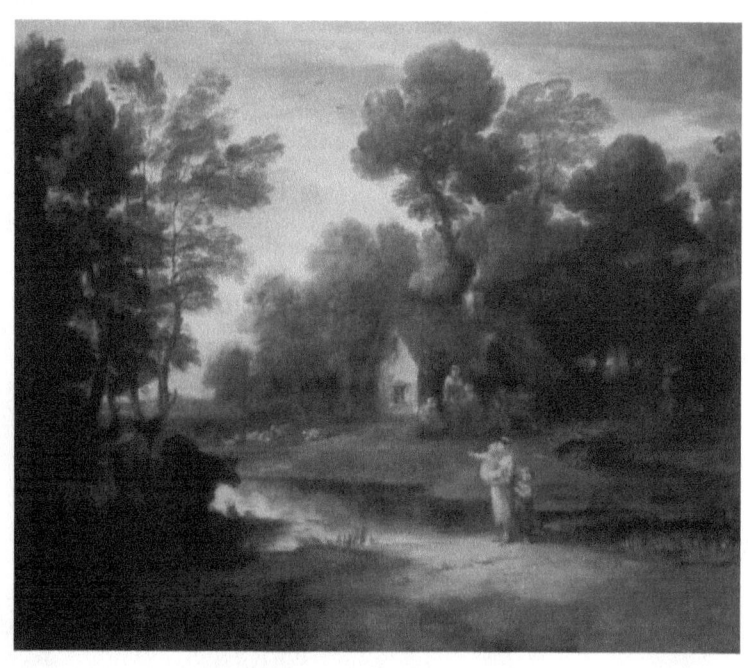

Wooded Landscape with Cattle by a Pool and a Cottage at Evening, 1782, oil on canvas

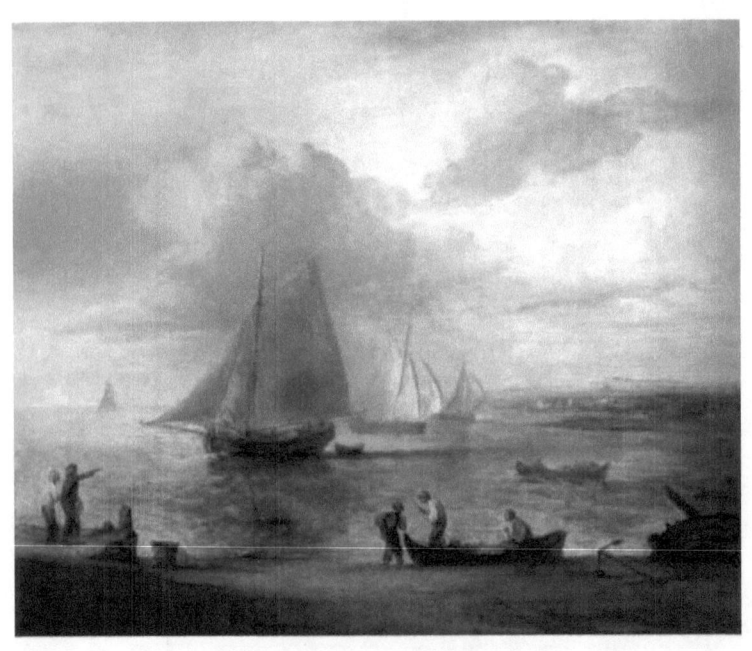

Coastal Scene, 1783, oil on canvas

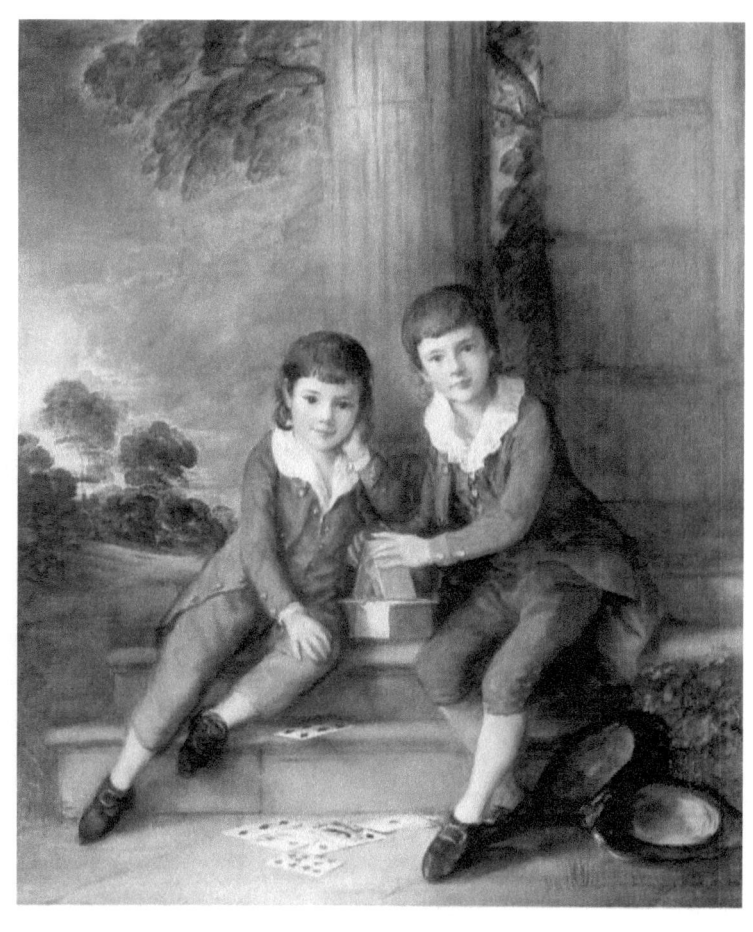

John and Henry Trueman Villebois, 1783, oil on canvas

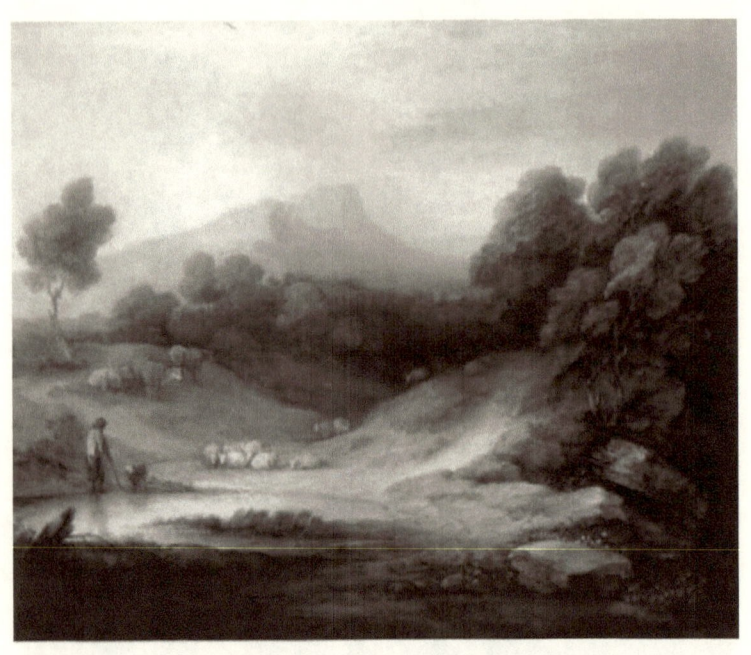

Mountain Landscape with Shepherd, 1783, oil on canvas

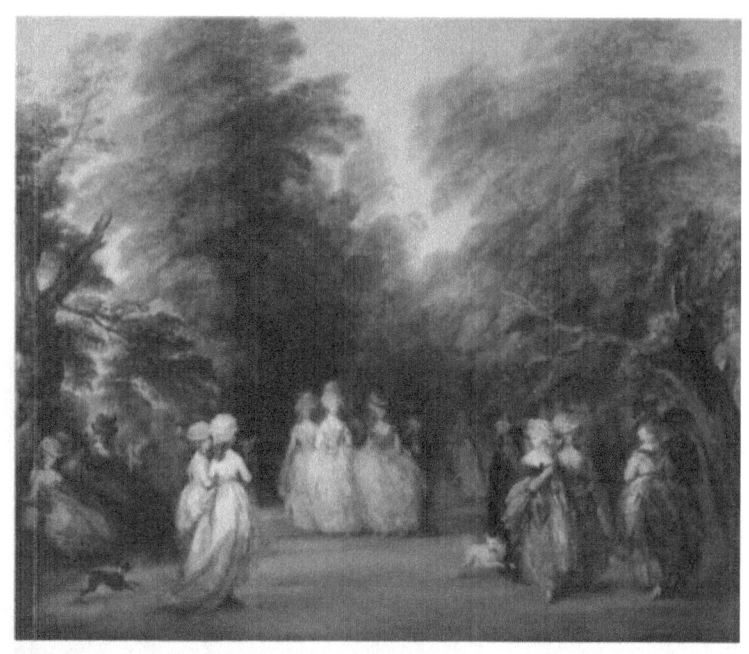

The Mall in St. James's Park, 1783, oil on canvas

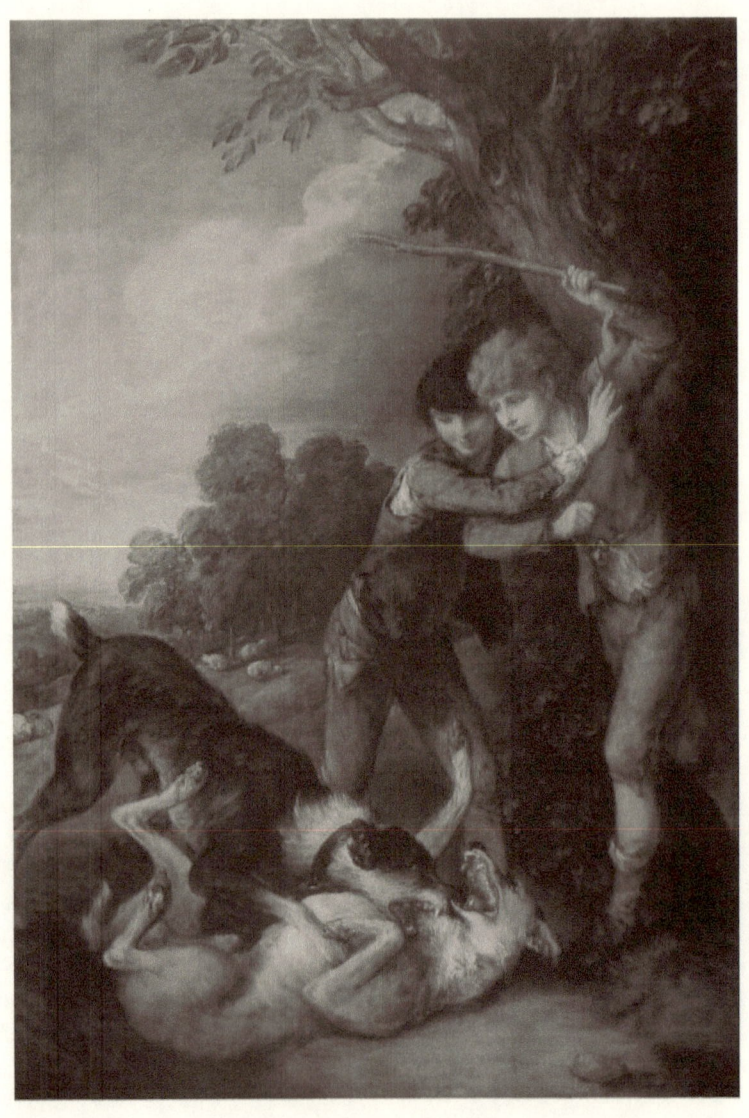

Two Shepherd Boys with Dogs Fighting, 1783, oil on canvas

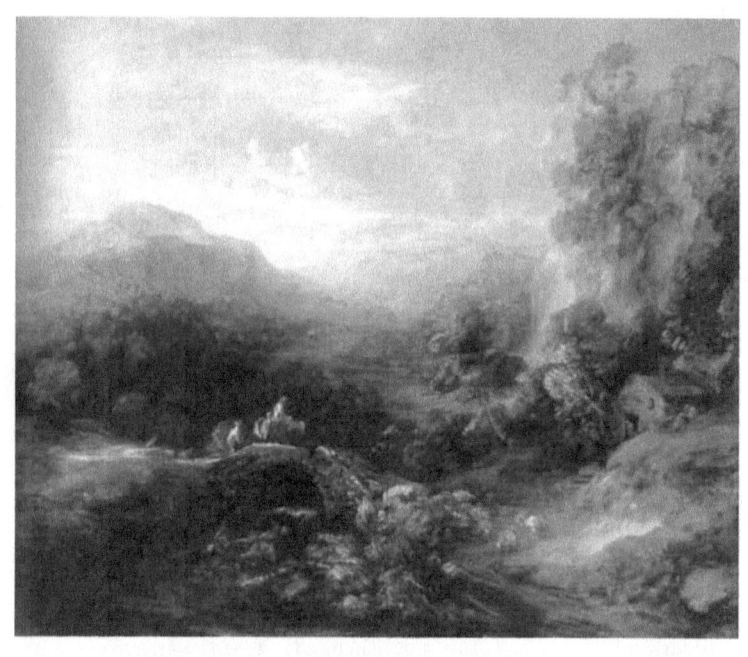

Mountain Landscape with Peasants Crossing a Bridge, 1784, oil on canvas

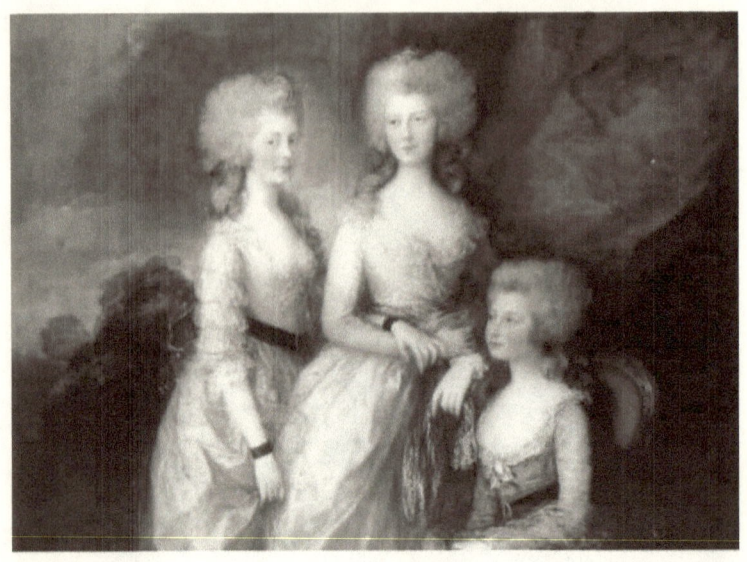

The three eldest daughters of George III: Princesses
Charlotte, Augusta and Elizabeth, 1784, oil on canvas

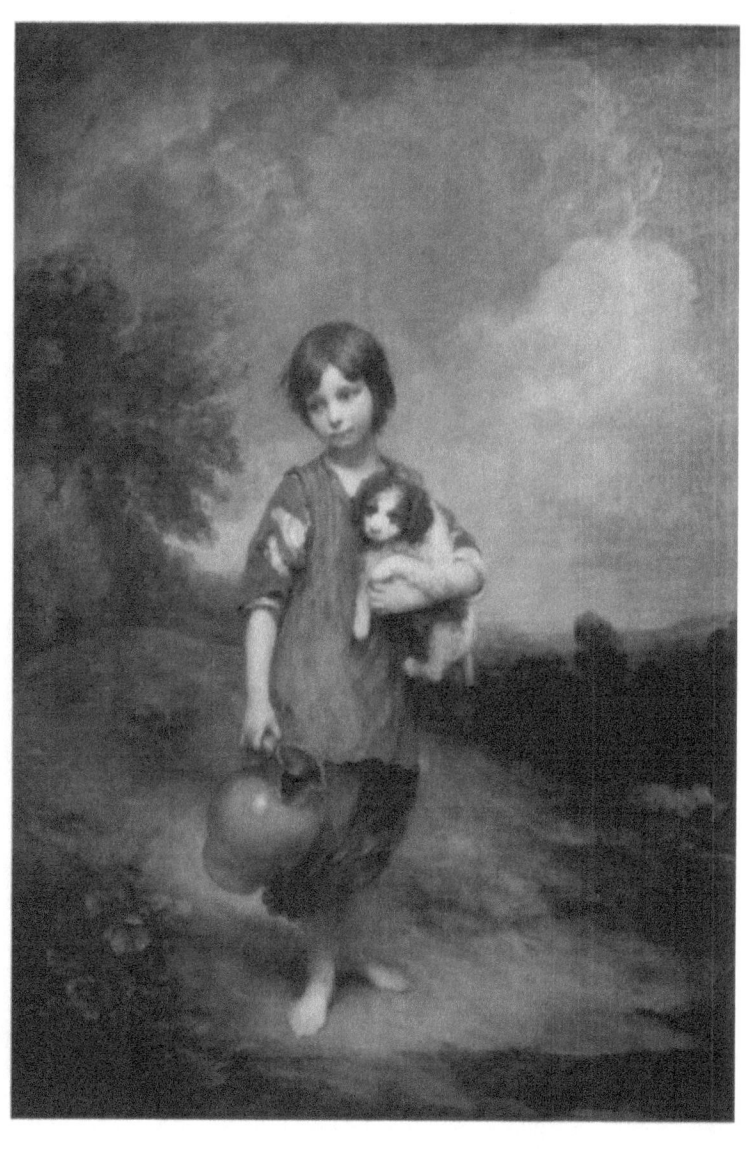

A peasant girl with dog and jug, 1785, oil on canvas

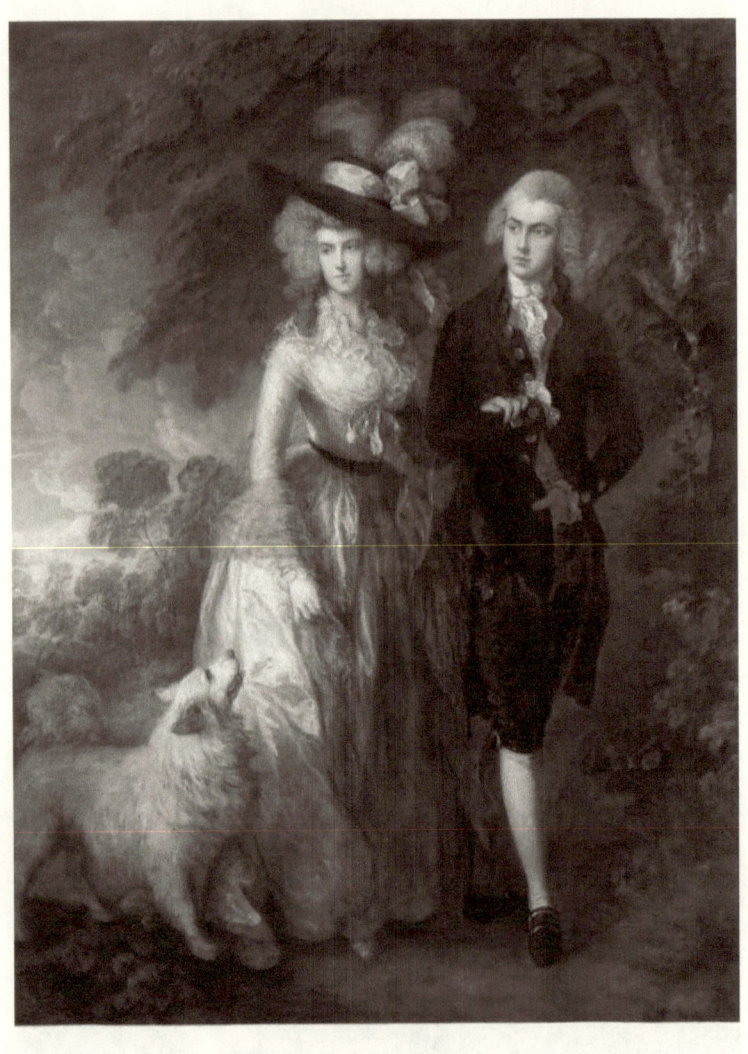

Mr. and Mrs. William Hallett (The Morning Walk),
1785, oil on canvas

Instinctive, unpompous, drawn to music and the theatre more than to literature or history, and to nature more than to anything, Gainsborough continues to enchant us, as the serious Reynolds seldom can. Suffolk-born, like Constable, he also became, within his means and times, a 'natural painter' - albeit of a very different kind. Although he said he wished nothing more than 'to take my Viol de Gamba and walk off to some sweet Village where I can paint Landskips', his feeling for nature encompassed much more than landscape. Children and animals, women and men, everything that dances, shimmers, breathes, whispers or sings, look natural in Gainsborough's enchanted world, so that 'nature' comes to encompass silks and gauzes, ostrich feathers and powdered hair as much as woods and ponds and butterflies. But this rapturous manner of painting, in which all parts of a canvas were worked on together with a flickering brush, only appears in mature works, such as this famous and splendid picture.

In his early years in Sudbury, after his training in London restoring Dutch landscapes and working with a French engraver, Gainsborough's finish was less free. After moving to the resort town of Bath in about 1759, he found a metropolitan clientele, and discovered Van Dyck in country-house collections. Both were to be decisive, and the effects are best judged in his portraits of women sitters, on the scale of life, in which elegance and ease of manner combine with a new, more tender colour range and a loosening of paint texture. In 1774 he moved permanently to London, where he built up a great portrait practice, but also began to paint imaginative 'fancy pictures' inspired by Murillo. He never aspired to 'history painting' in the Grand Manner. His poetry resides mainly in his brush, not in compositional inventiveness.

It was surely Gainsborough's own inclination, however, to interpret a formal marriage portrait, for which the sitters probably sat separately, as a parkland promenade. William Hallett was 21 and his wife Elizabeth, nñe Stephen, 20 when they solemnly linked arms to walk in step together through life. A Spitz dog paces at their side, right foot forward like theirs, as pale and fluffy as Mrs Hallet is pale and gauzy. Being only a dog with no sense of occasion he pants joyfully hoping for attention. The parkland is a painted backdrop, like those of Victorian photographers, yet it provides a pretext for depicting urban sitters in urban finery as if in the dappled light of a world fresh with dew.

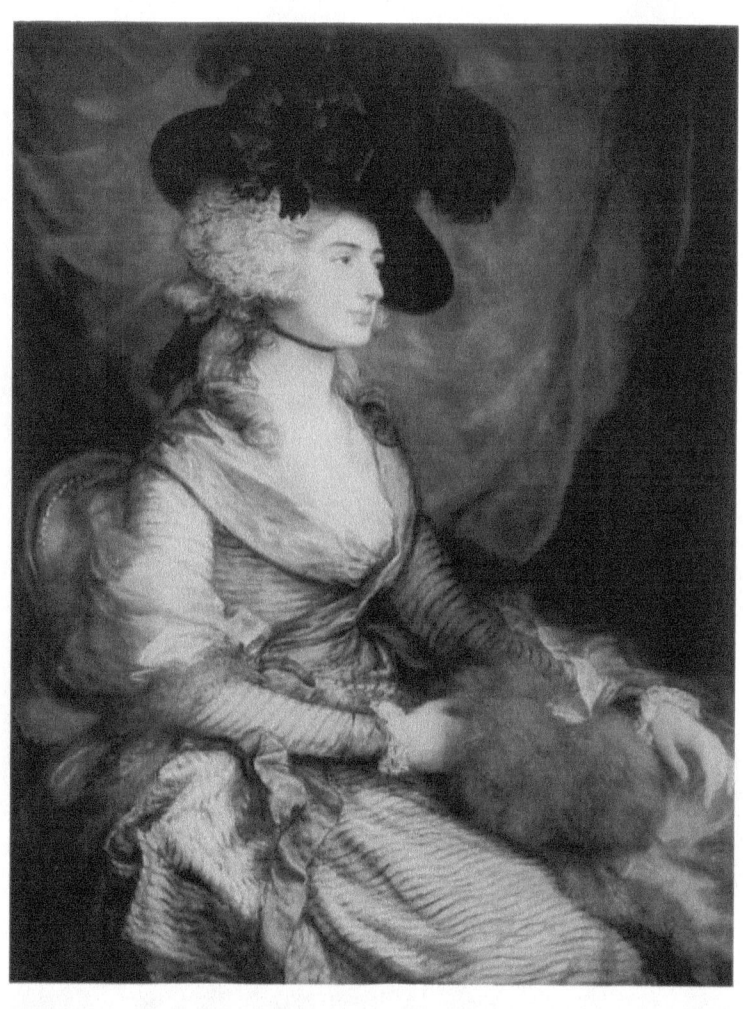

Mrs. Sarah Siddons, the actress, 1785, oil on canvas

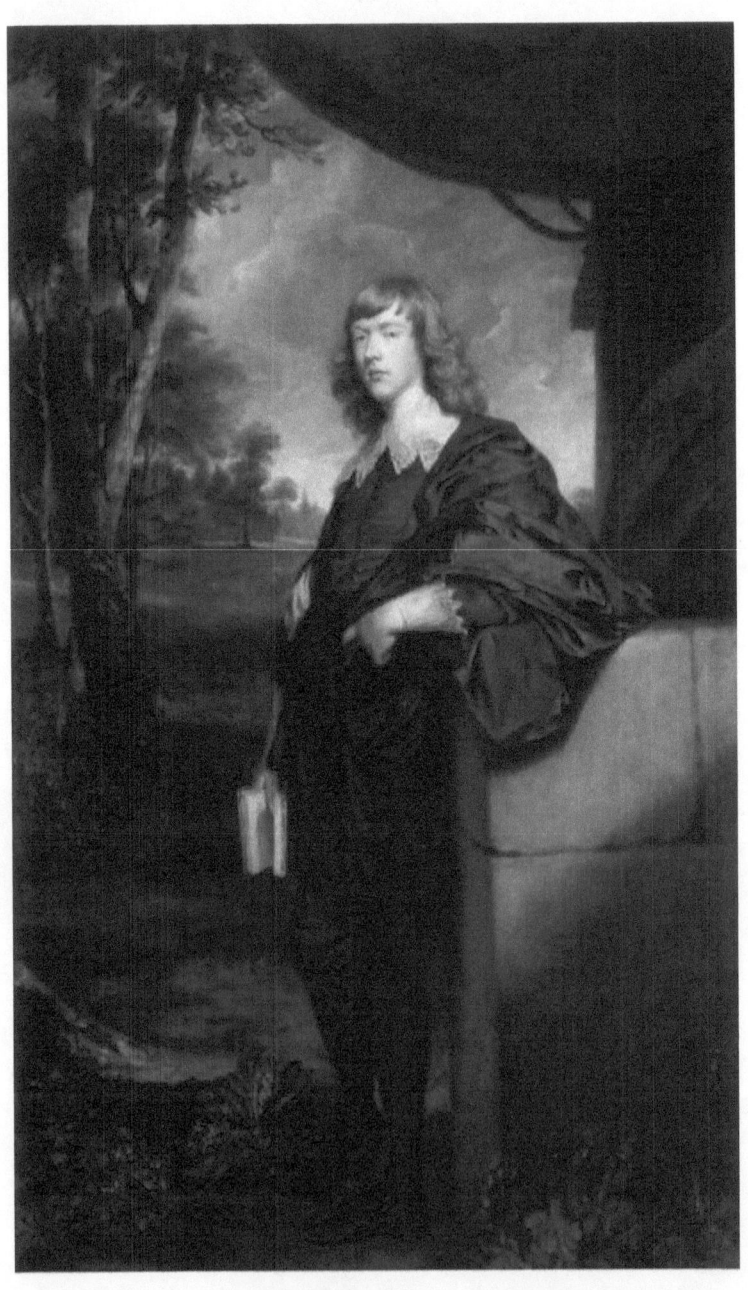

Portrait of George Spencer, 2nd Earl Spencer, c.1785, oil

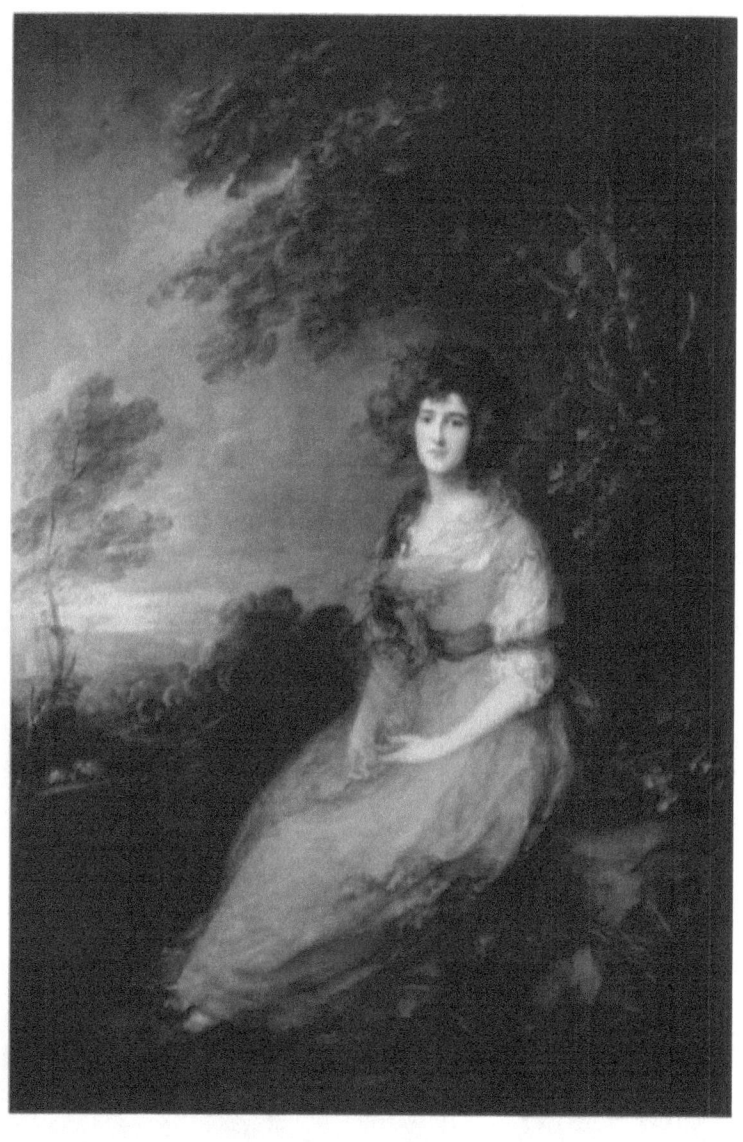

Mrs. Richard Brinsley Sheridan, 1786, oil on canvas

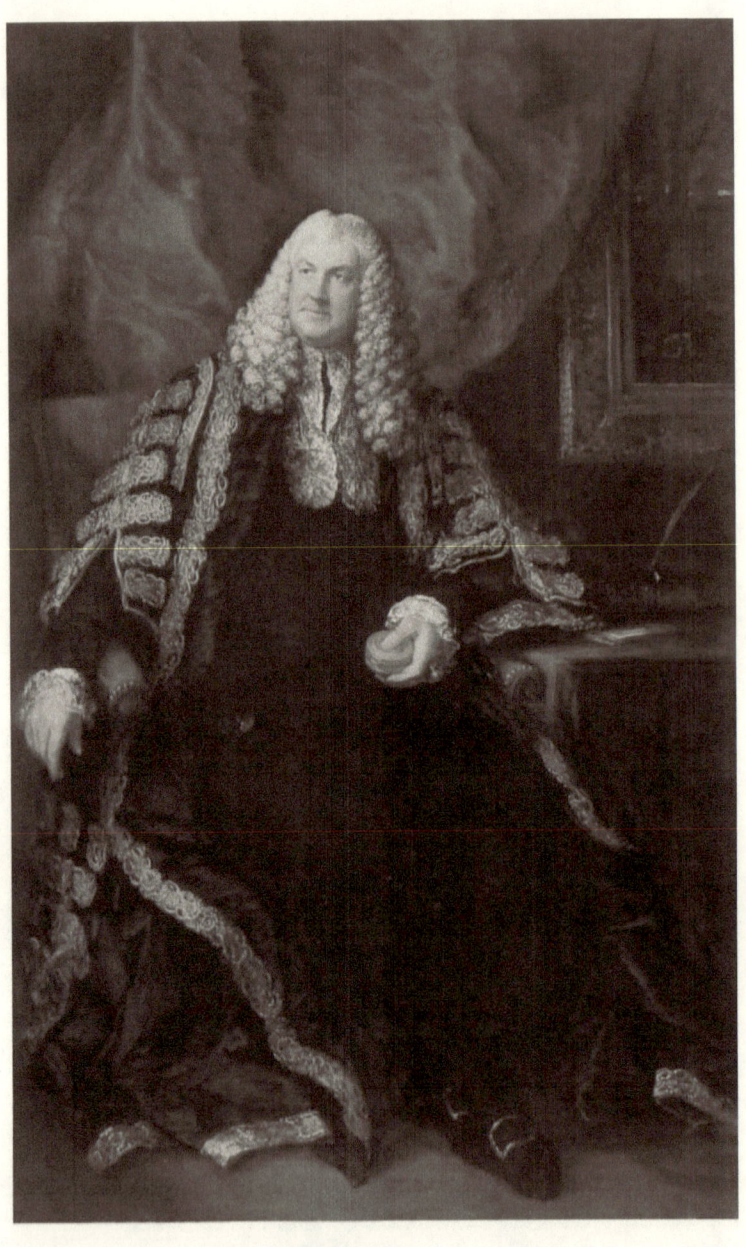

The Honourable Charles Wolfran Cornwal, 1786, oil on canvas

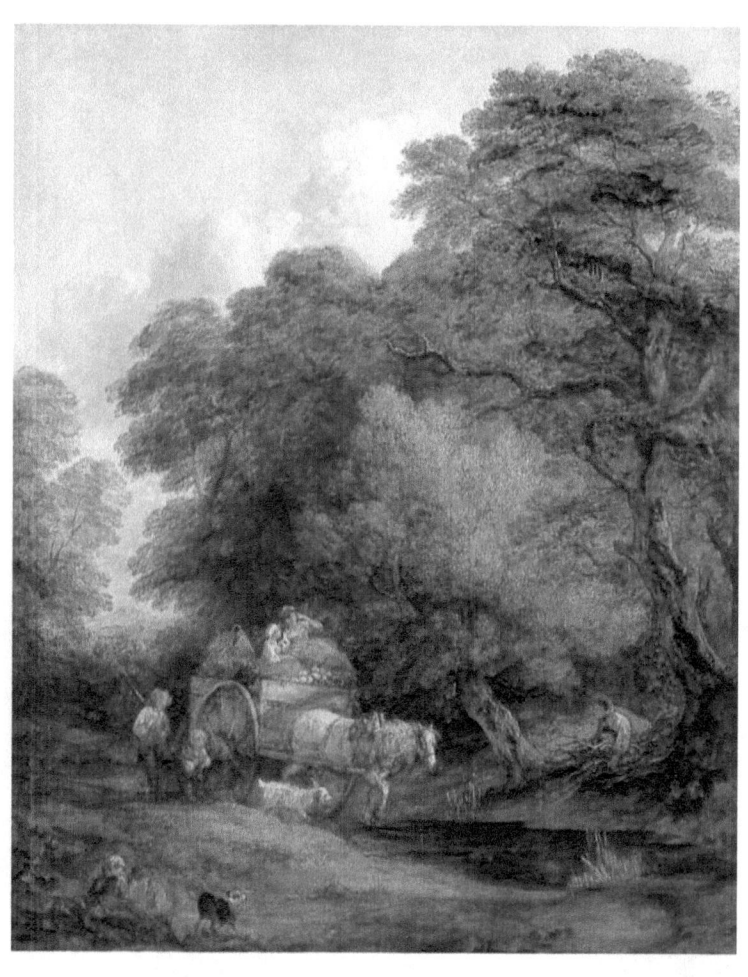

The market cart, 1786, oil on canvas

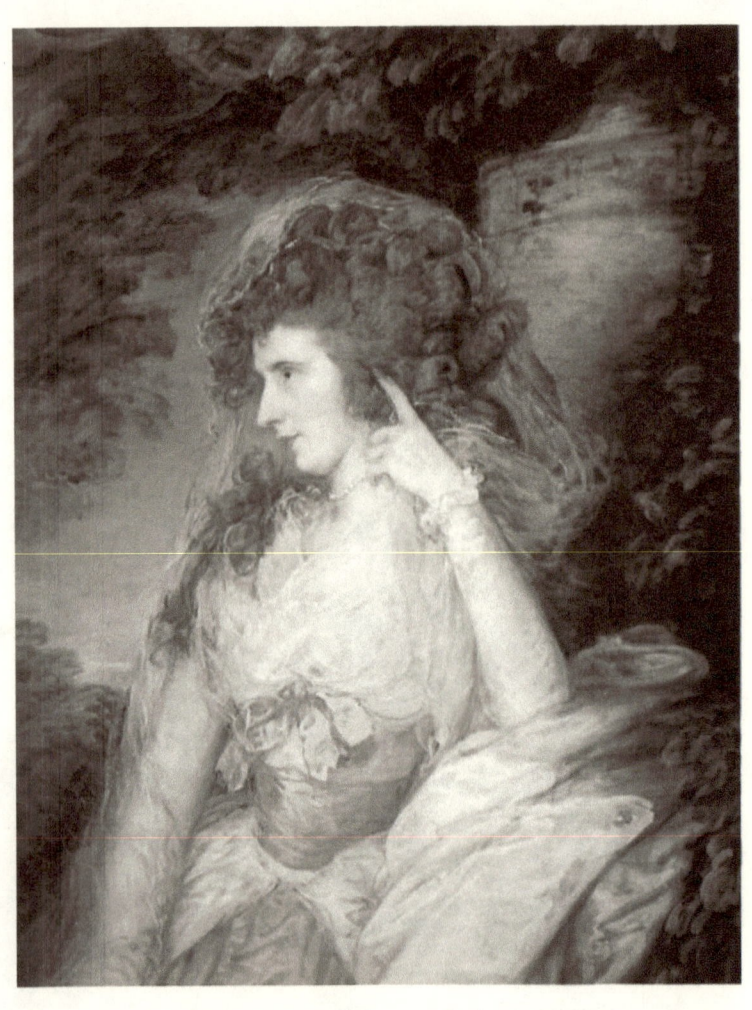

Mary, Lady Bate Dudley, 1787, oil on canvas

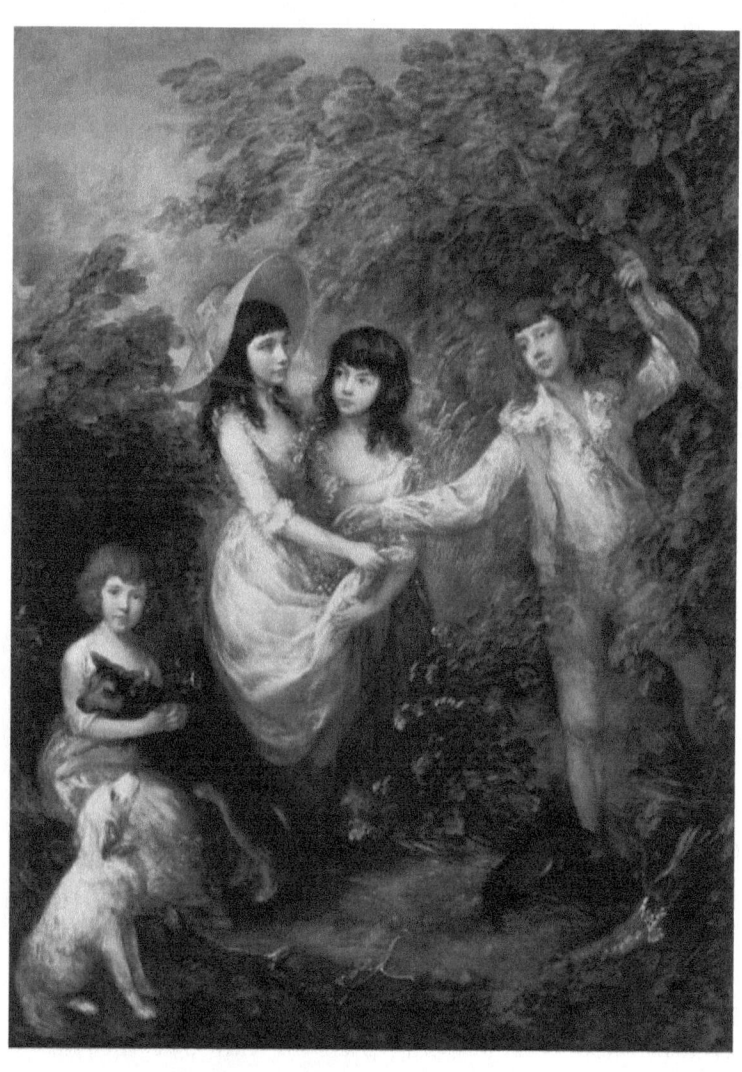

The Marsham Children, 1787, oil on canvas,

In the Rococo period all over Europe Watteau stood as symbol of a new gracefulness and ease: the proof that the painter can tackle apparently flippant subject-matter and yet be a great artist. Watteau's own attitude was soon to matter no longer; he represented something which he might not always have wished to be. His compositions exercised an influence which was perhaps sometimes hardly conscious. A Frenchified grace in genre subjects was attempted everywhere, even in England.

The most personal response to Watteau is in Gainsborough, a great painter who yet seldom painted anything resembling a Watteau subject. Several of Gainsborough's early portraits show him utilizing Watteau's compositions for his sitters. But Gainsborough borrows more than a pose, as his later pictures confirm. It is freedom that exhales from his portraits: the freedom of nature and natural settings is allied to free handling, and the whole expresses the idiosyncratic character of his sitters, so relaxed and yet lively, just like Gainsborough's own nature. The painter who described himself in a letter to a patron as 'but a wild goose at best' was dearly Watteau's cousin, taking the same freedom for the artist as he expressed in his art, and conscious of being the odd man out in ordinary society. Gainsborough, if anyone, was the heir to Watteau's art, but he was not to turn to the 'fancy picture' until late in life; and there would have been little patronage for an English painter producing fêtes galantes in preference to portraits.

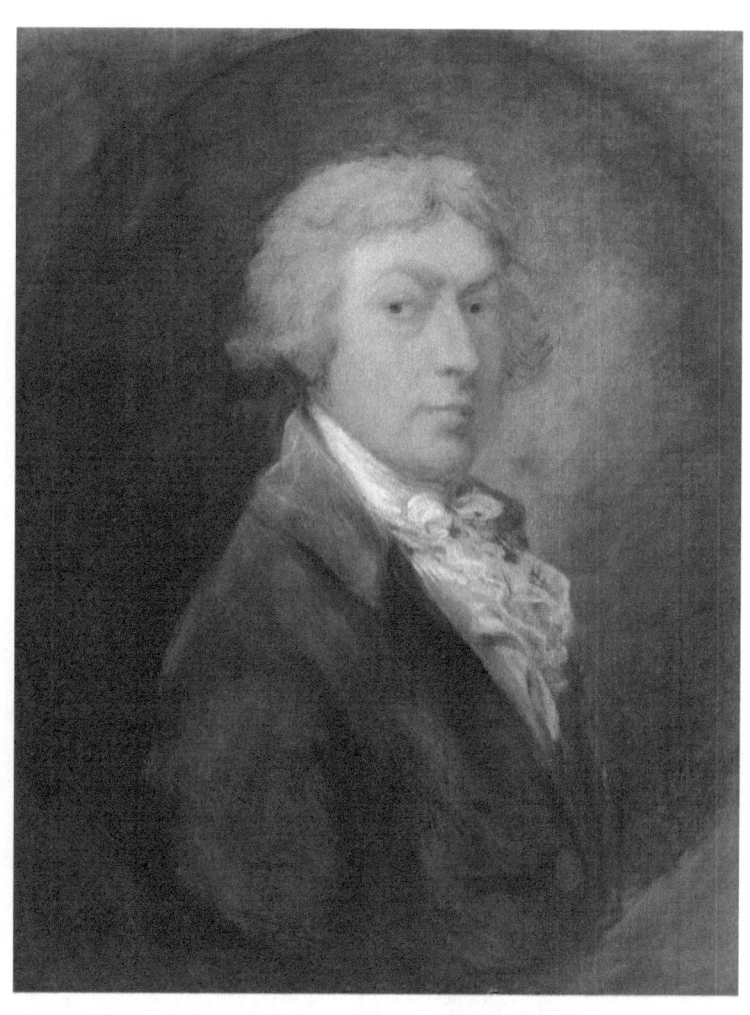

Self-Portrait, 1787, oil on canvas

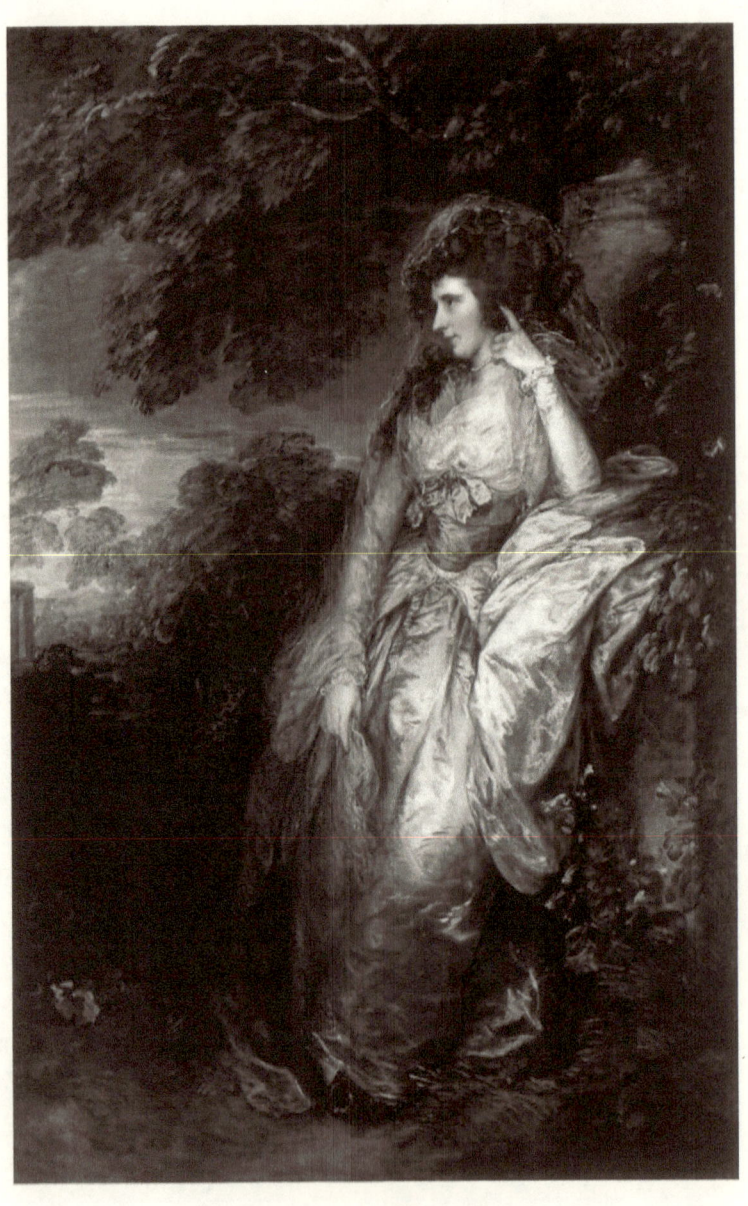

Lady Bate-Dudley, 1787, oil on canvas

Lady Bate-Dudley was the wife of the newspaper publisher and art critic Sir Henry Bate-Dudley who since 1777 had been giving Gainsborough enthusiastic support in his articles. In 1780 he had the artist paint a life-size portrait of himself in a park landscape. When the portrait of his wife followed in 1787, Gainsborough once again chose the landscape situation, but had recourse to a classical Urania pose.

Lady Bate-Dudley is leaning against a garden monument with her legs crossed. The extended index finger of her left hand is touching her temple, a graceful, relaxed pose. In England, a natural form of dress had already by now become usual. Flowing around the body is a diaphanous veil which covers her coiffure. Her hair itself is no longer powdered, while skirts were only slightly "upholstered" and fabrics were allowed to fall loosely and playfully. The decollete was smaller, the bodice less rigid, and there was only a shawl about the hips. This new naturalness is the hallmark of Lady Bate-Dudley's portrait. Gainsborough creates a virtuoso combination of this natural portraiture and the trees and shrubs of the garden ambience. The ensemble is supported by the interplay of the distant light with the close-up illumination. Lady Bate-Dudley appears as her own source of light in the picture.

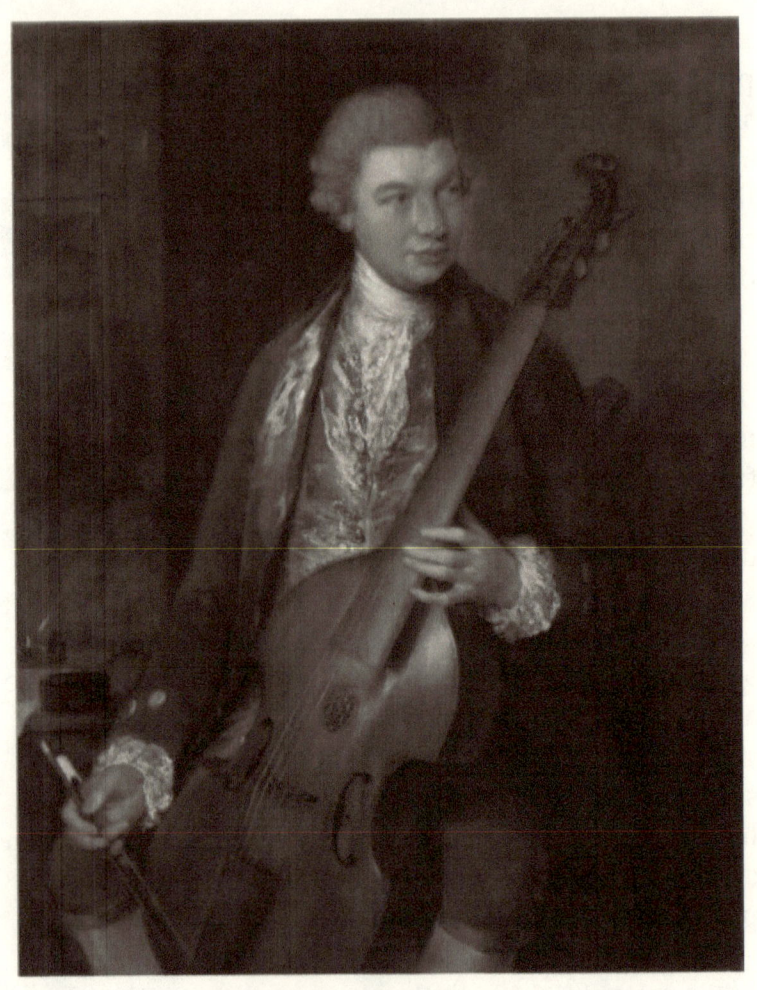

Carl Friedrich Abel, oil on canvas

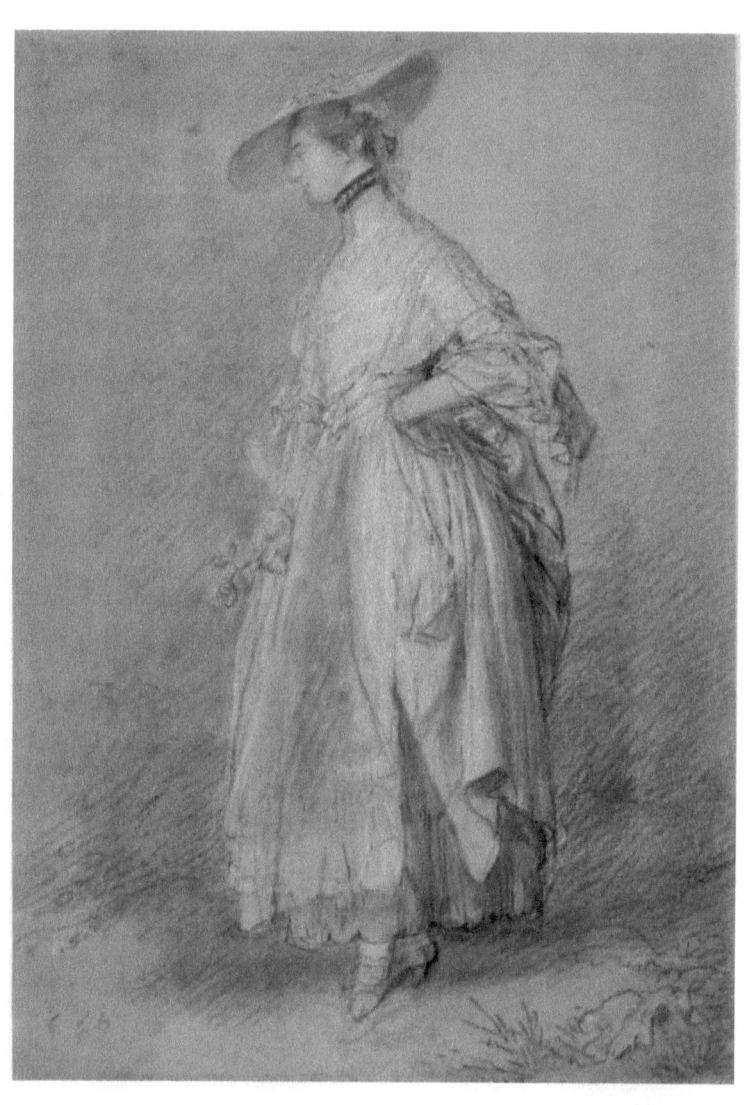

A woman with a rose, chalk, stump

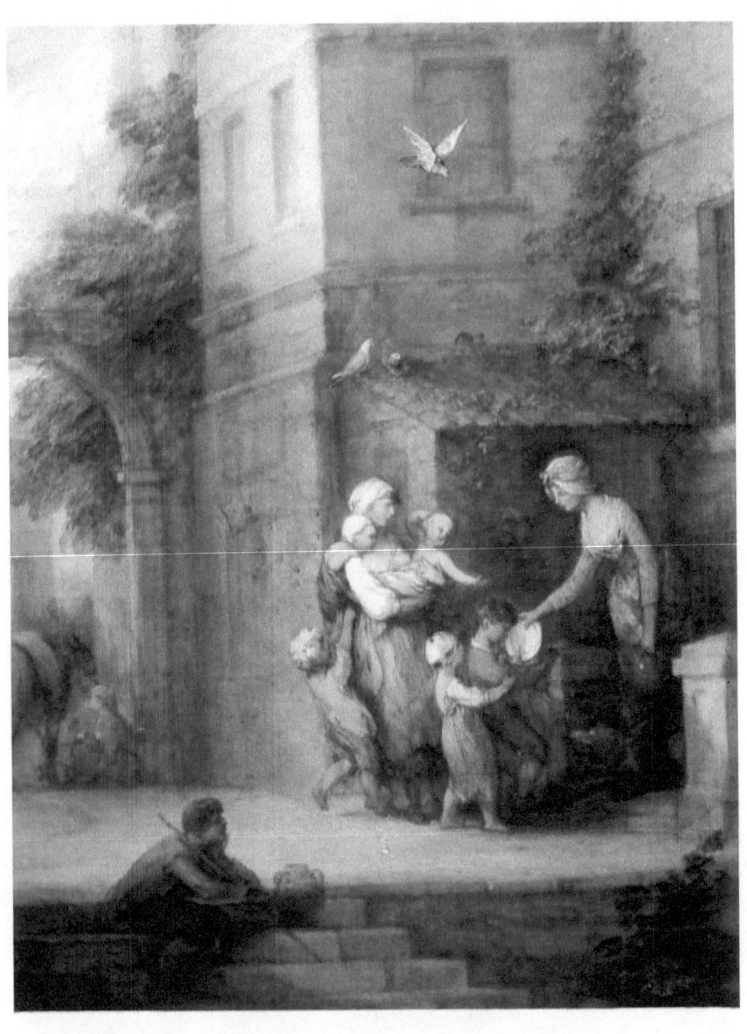

Charity relieving Distress, oil on canvas

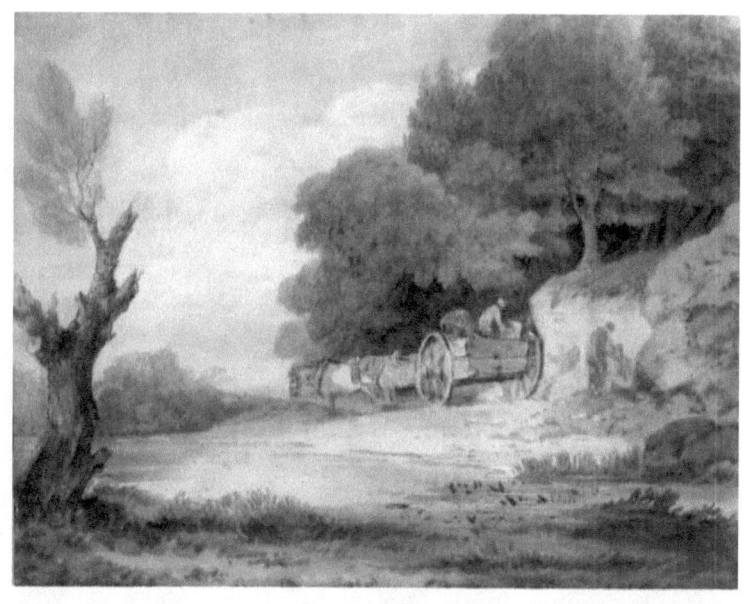

Figures with cart at roadside, wash, chalk, graphite

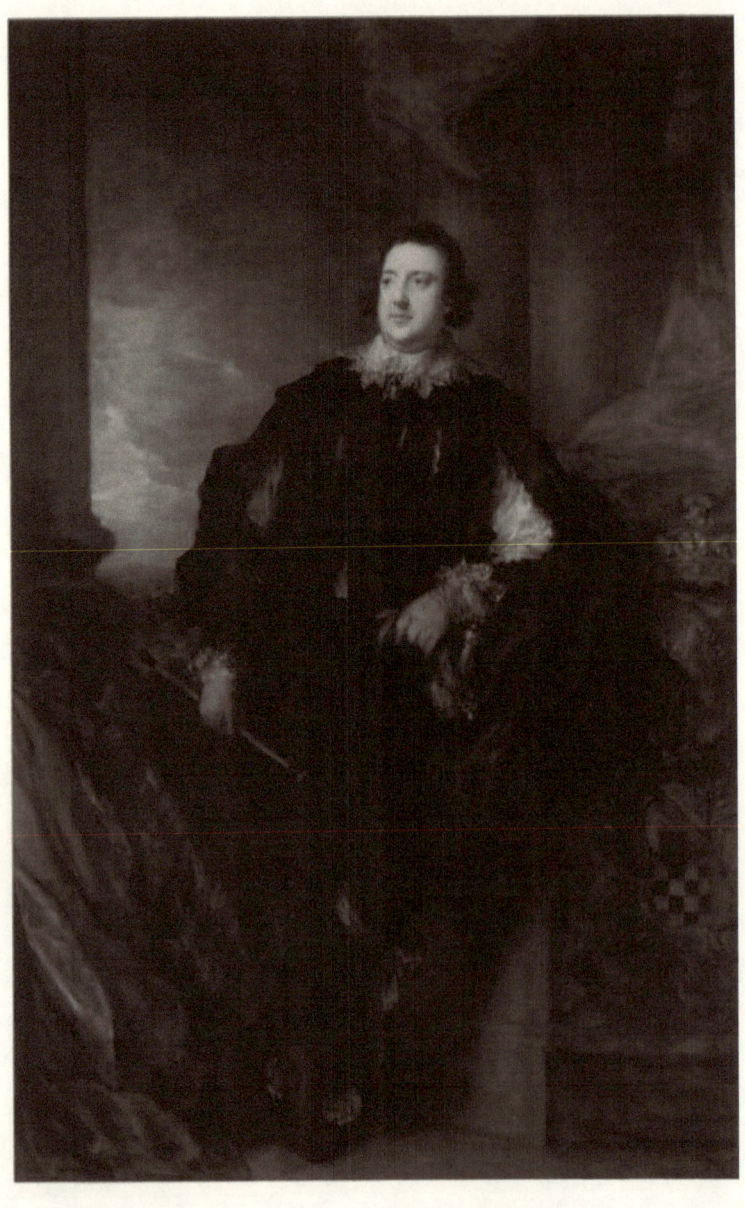

Charles Howard, 11th Duke of Norfolk, oil on canvas

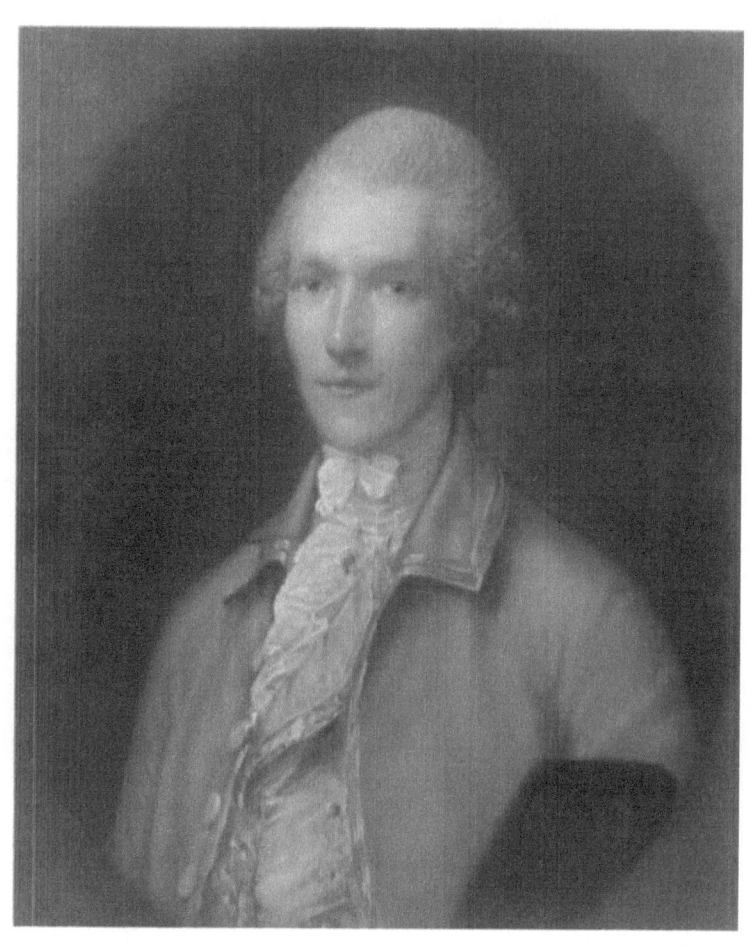

Count Rumford, oil on canvas

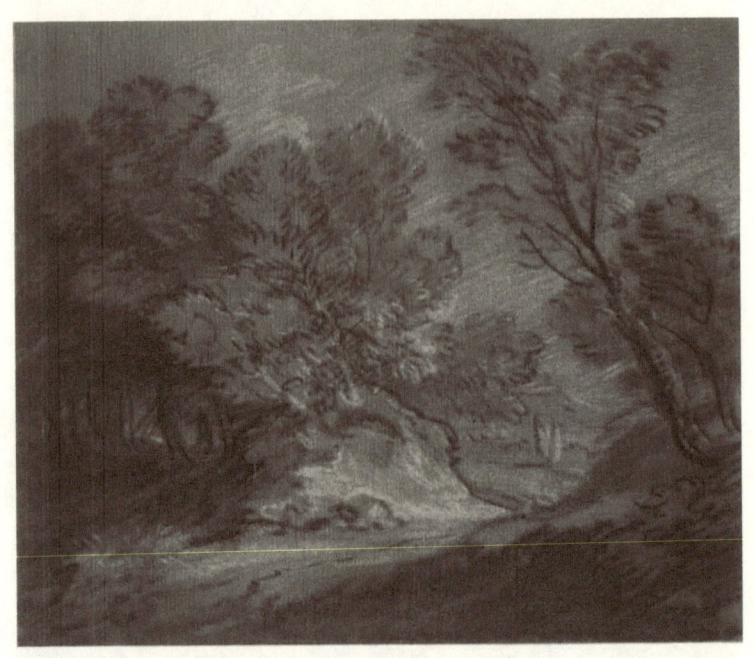

Forest landscape with mountain, chalk

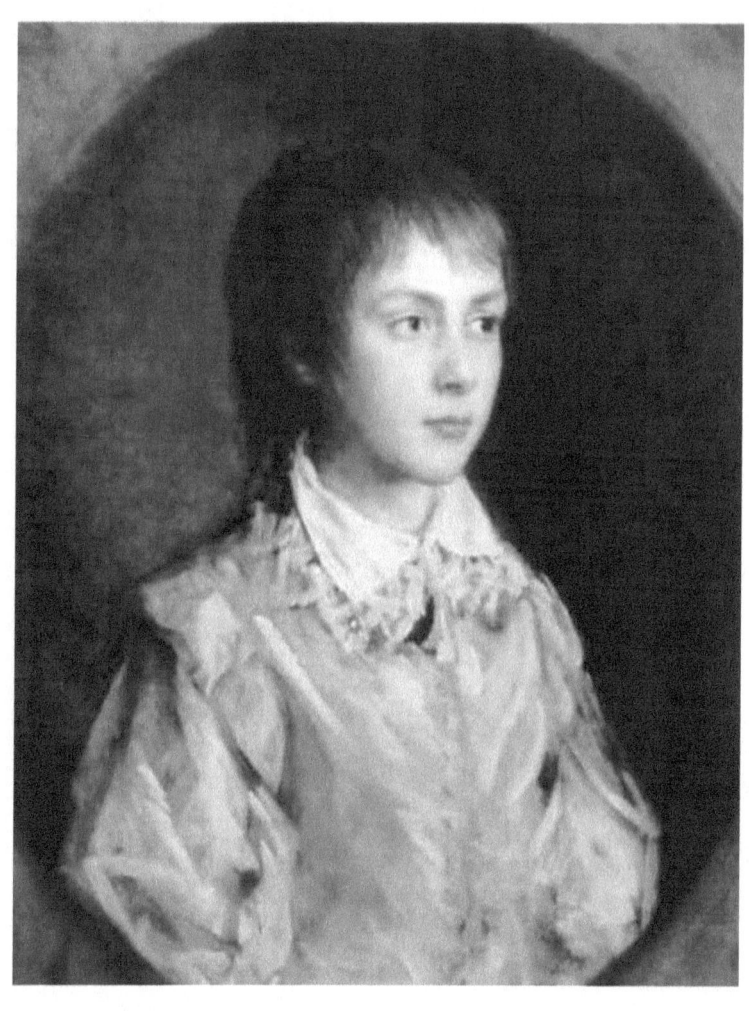

Edward Richard Gardiner, oil on canvas

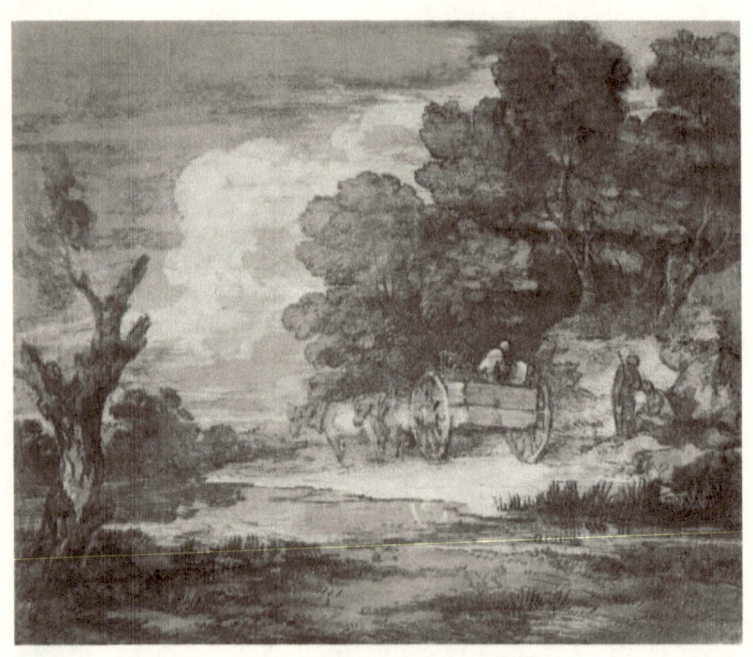

Landscape

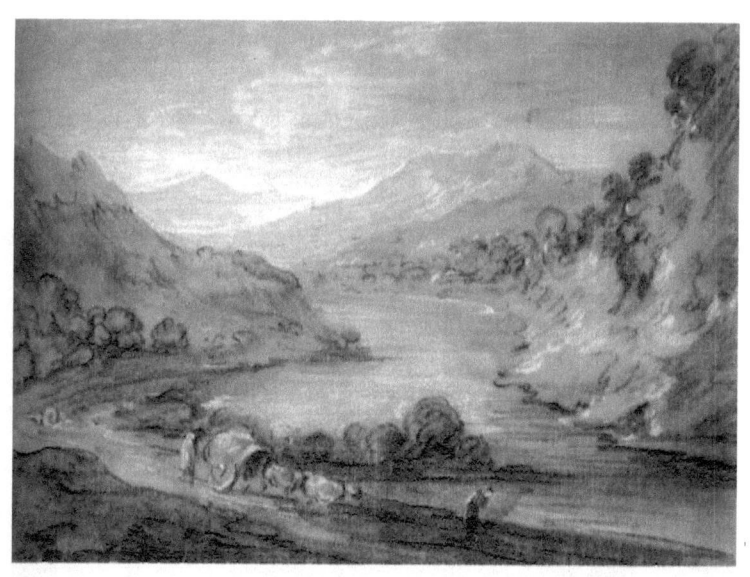

Mountainous Landscape with Cart And Figures, chalk

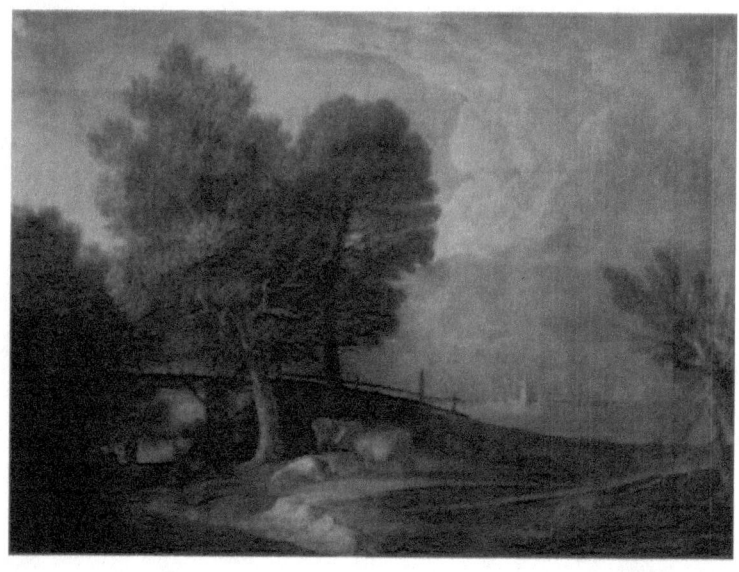

Figures with Cattle in a Landscape, oil on canvas

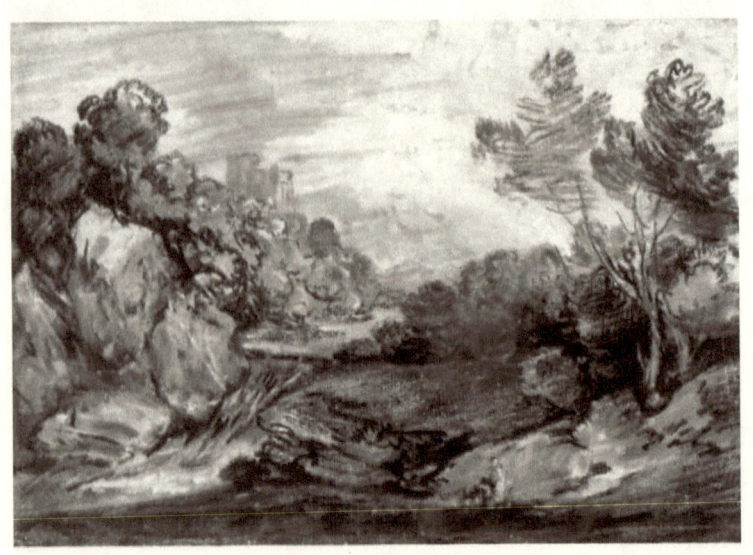

Rocky wooded landscape with waterfall, castle and
mountain, chalk, stump

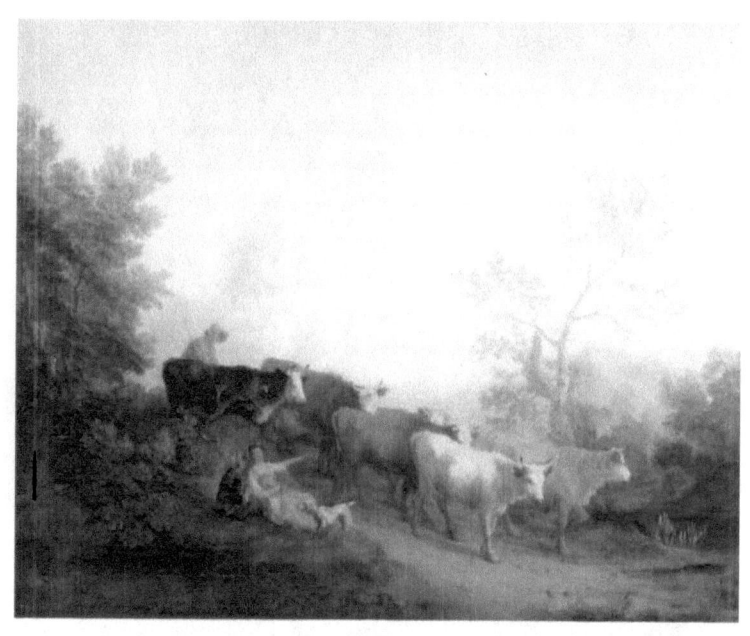

Homecoming, oil on canvas

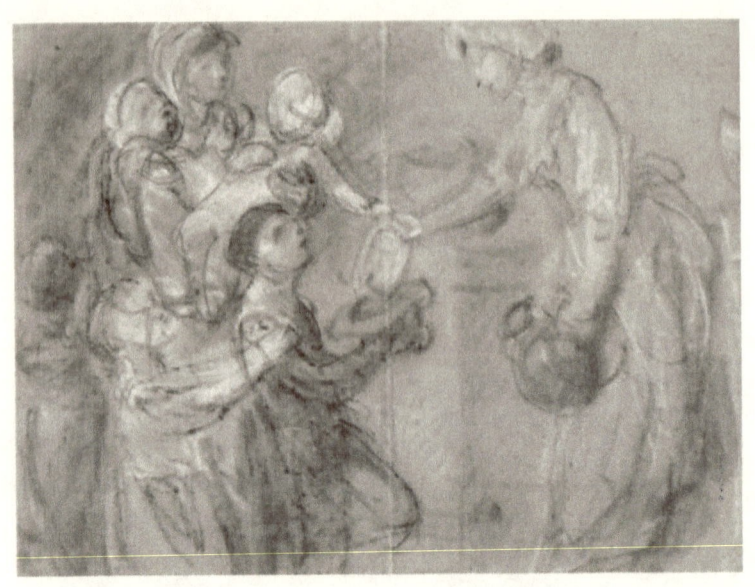

Study For "Charity Relieving Distress", chalk

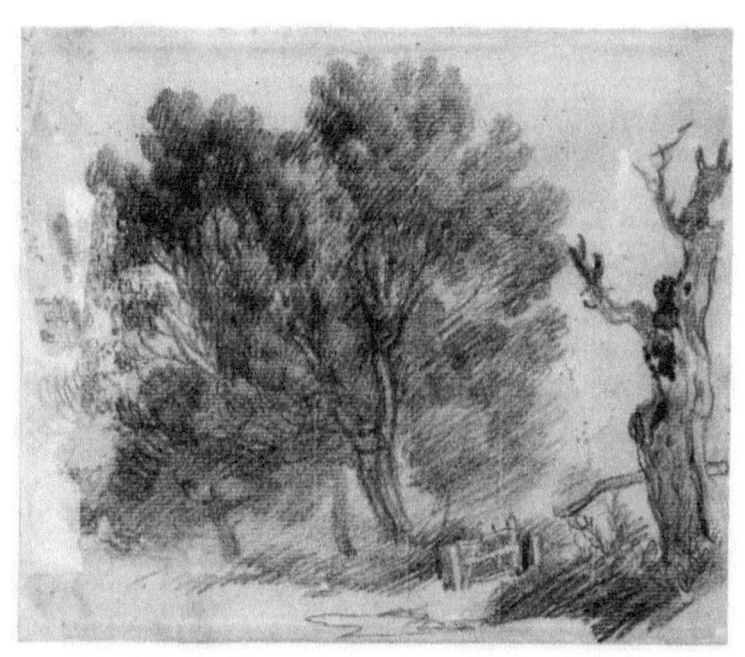

Study of willows, graphite

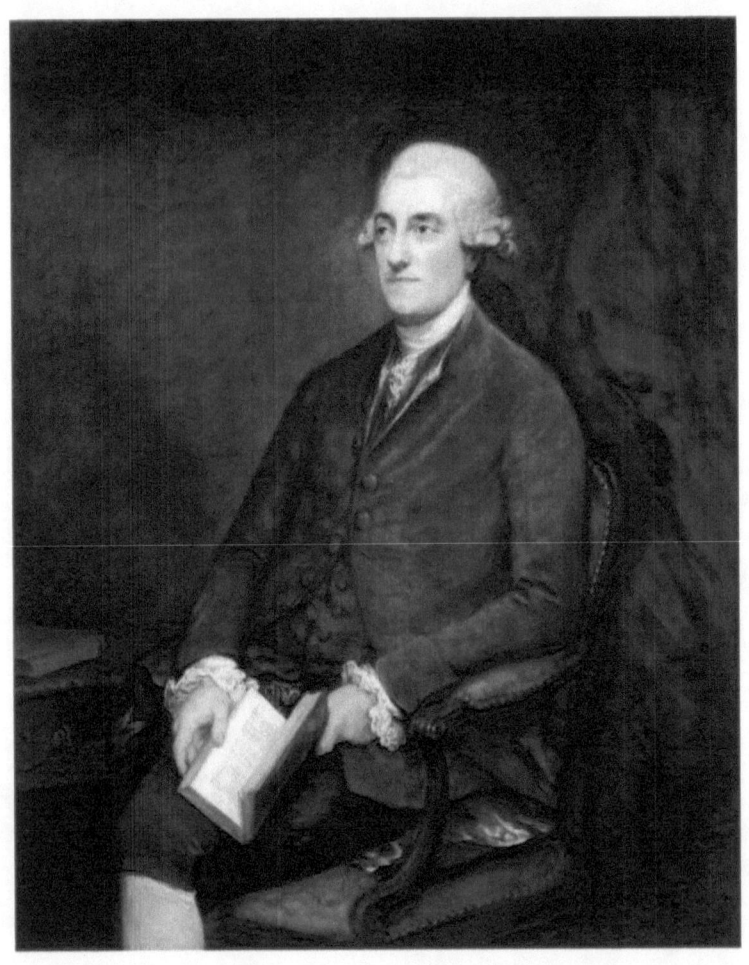

Isaac Henrique Sequeira, oil on canvas

Isaac Henrique Sequeira was the physician of the painter Gainsborough. The refined style of this portrait comes close to that of Van Dyck as a reminder of his long stay at the English court.

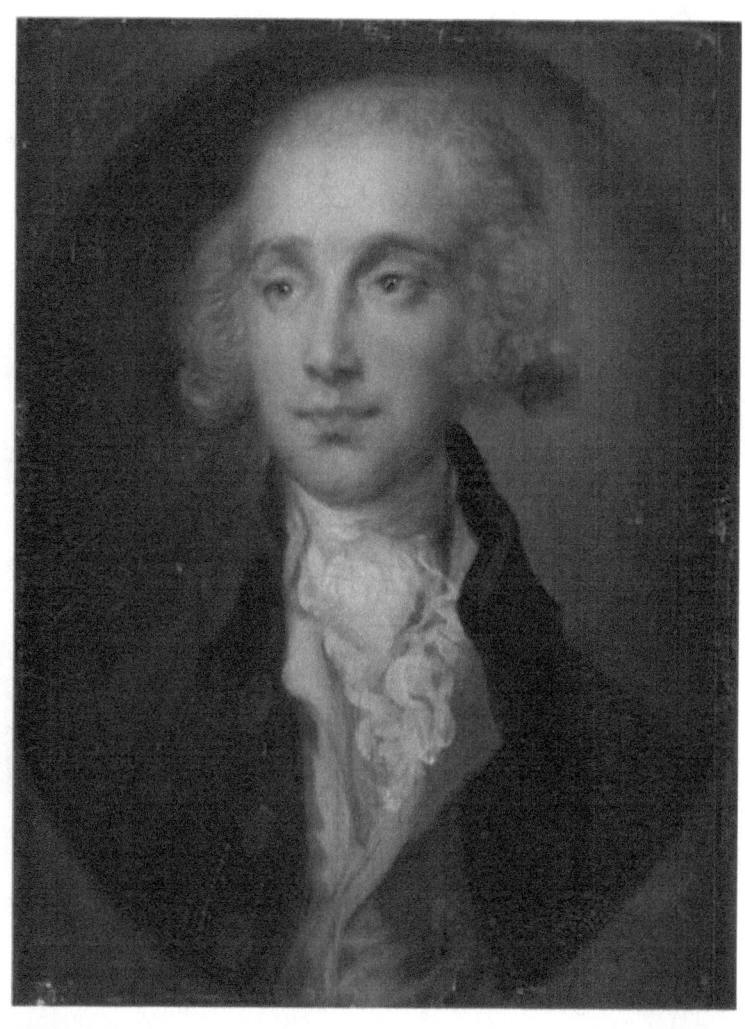

James Maitland, 8th Earl of Lauderdale, oil on canvas

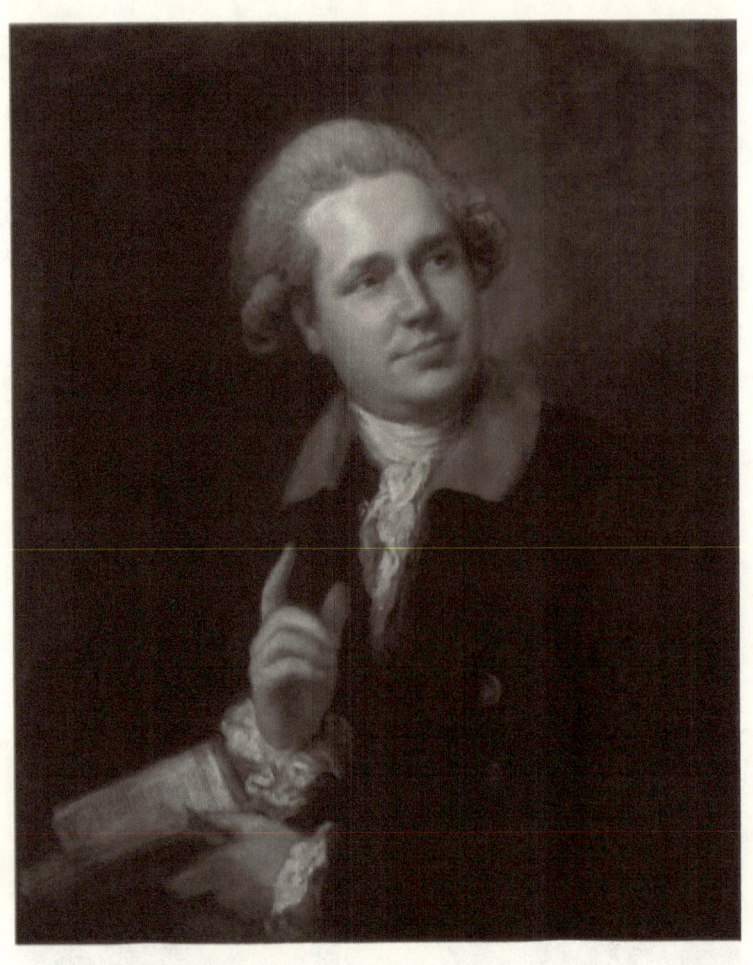

John Henderson, oil on canvas

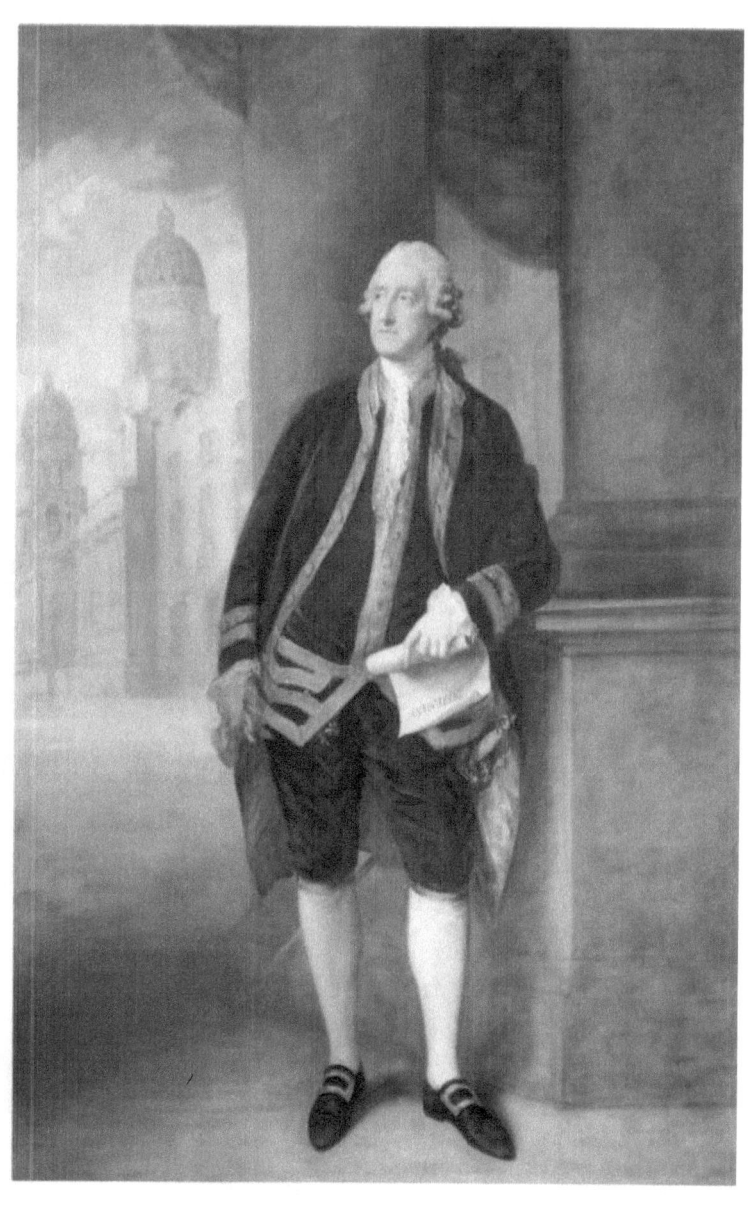

John Montagu, 4th Earl of Sandwich, oil on canvas

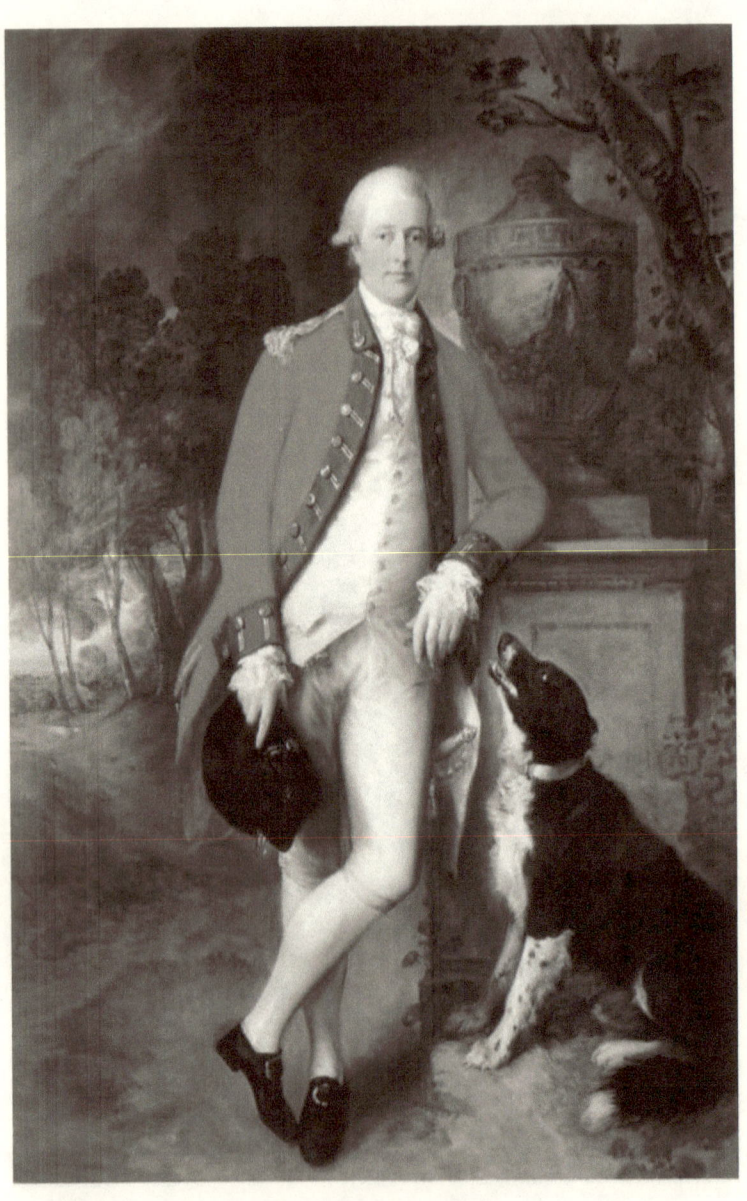

Portrait of Colonel John Bullock, oil on canvas

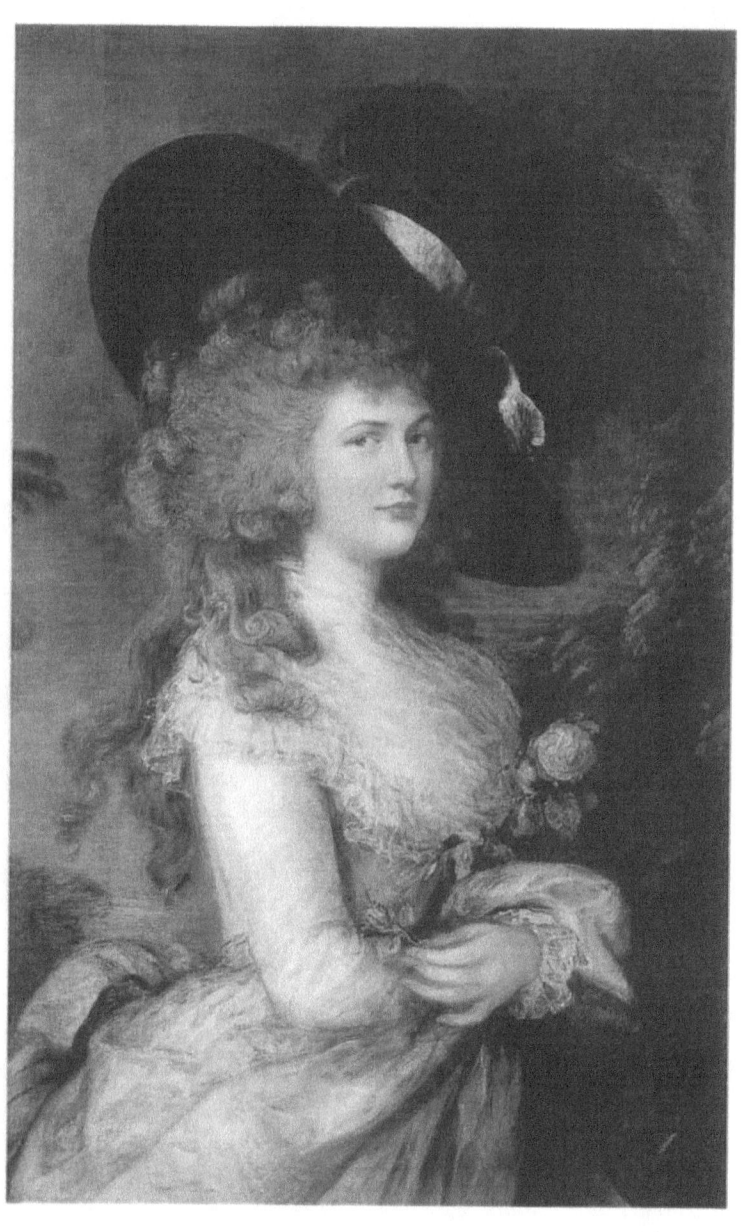

Portrait of Georgiana, Duchess of Devonshire, oil on canvas

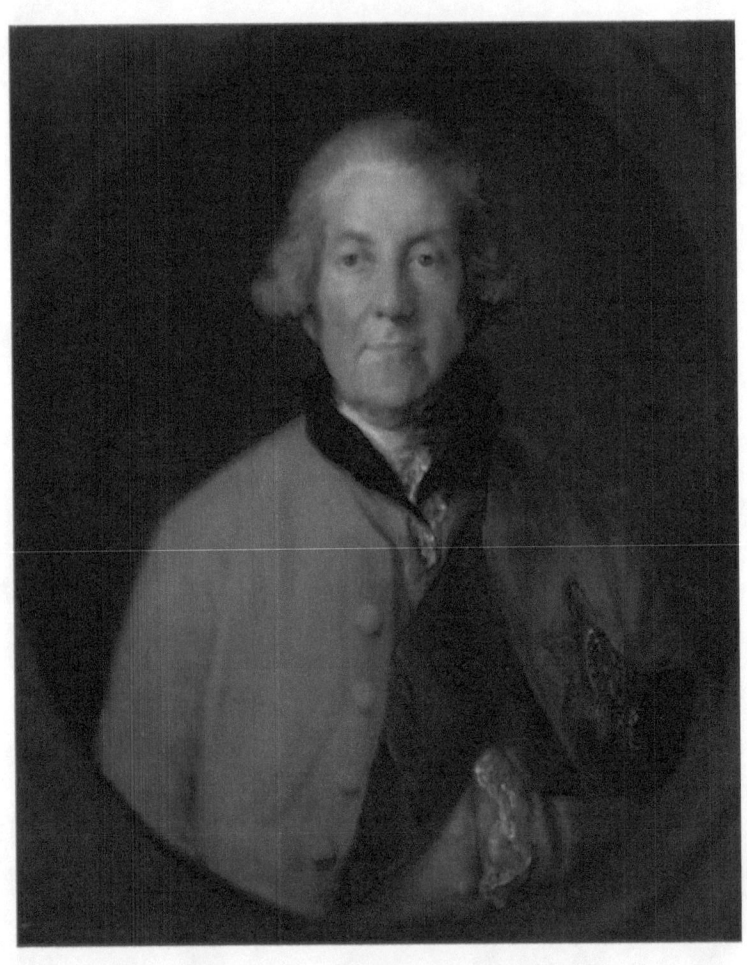

Portrait of John Russell, 4th Duke of Bedford, oil on canvas

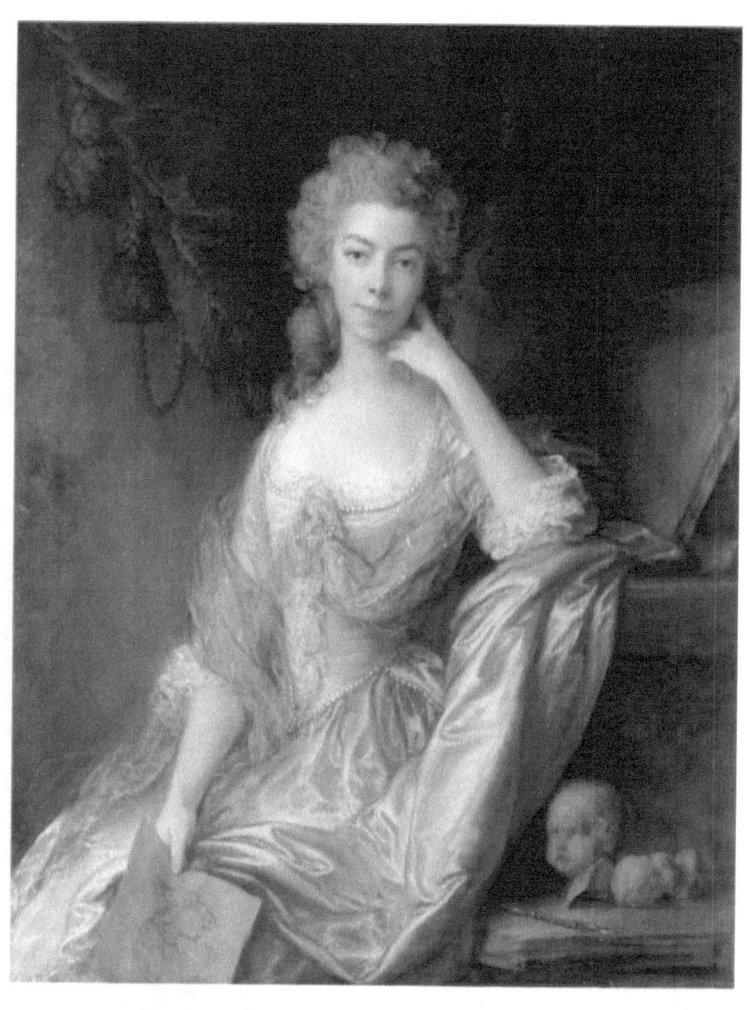

Portrait of Mrs. Drummond, oil on canvas

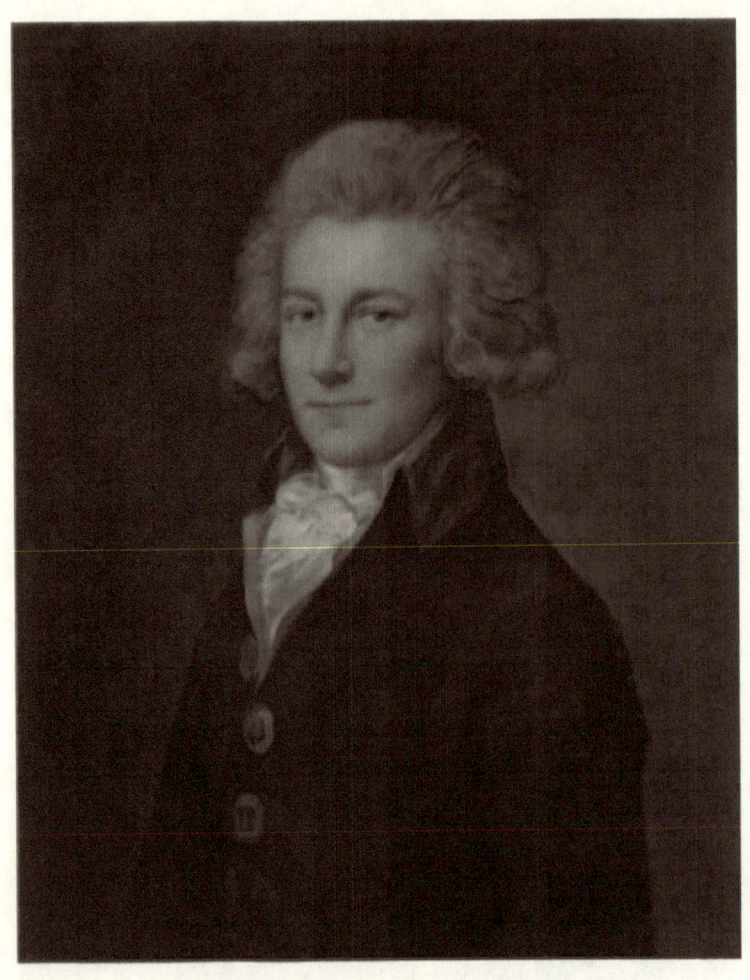

Portrait of Peter Godfrey of Old Hall East Bergholt
Suffolk, oil on canvas

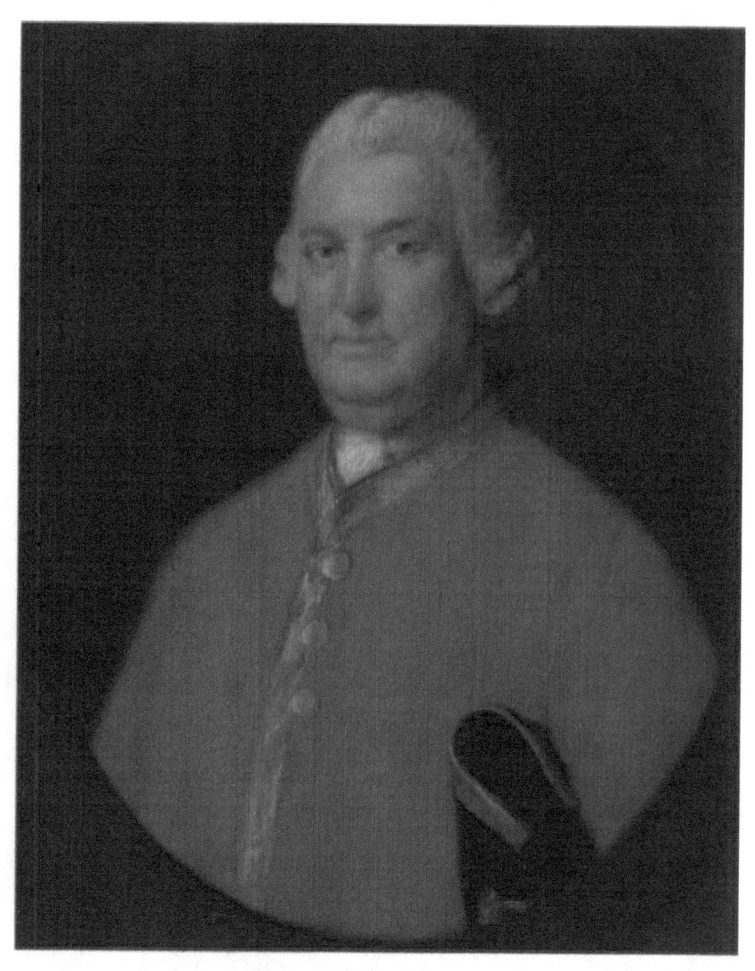

WC Stringer Lawrence, oil on canvas

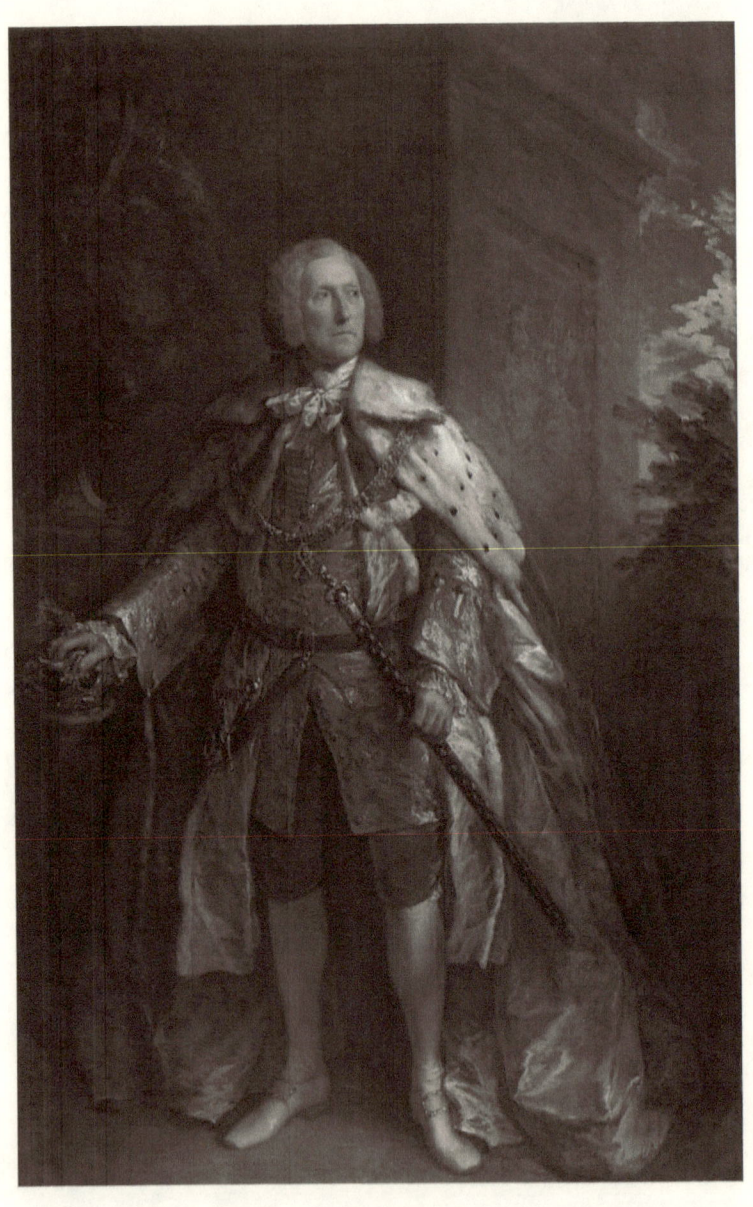

John Campbell, 4th Duke of Argyll, oil